PURPLE CHALKBOARD ACT PREP GUIDE

RENEE J. JANZEN

Copyright © 2015 Renee J. Janzen
All rights reserved.
ISBN: 069247773X
ISBN-13: 978-0692477731

DEDICATION

With gratitude to my former ACT students. Though you are too many to mention, your names, your faces, and your stories are etched on every page of this book. Thank you for your confidence, for trusting me with a bit of your future. I'll be watching with eager anticipation to see God's glory shine through your lives.

CONTENTS

	Acknowledgments	i
	Score Conversion Chart	ii
	Progress Chart	iii
1	Introduction to the ACT	Pg 5
2	Understanding the Reading Test	Pg 26
3	Understanding the Science Test	Pg 42
4	Understanding the English Test	Pg 64
5	Understanding the Math Test	Pg 81
6	Practice Math Test	Pg 94
7	Practice Math Test Answer Key and Explanations	Pg 122
8	Understanding the Writing Test (Optional)	Pg 154
9	The Week Before the Test	Pg 159
10	A Quick and Easy Guide to Getting Into and Paying for College	Pg 161

ACKNOWLEDGMENTS

The following four folks made up a one-stop publication crew: Micah Janzen, the Master Mathematician, Grace Janzen, the Graphics Guru, U.S. Air Force Pilot Sam Janzen served as a powerful prayer warrior, Natalie Janzen, who nobly navigated through every detail with a smile on her face. You all made it happen!

Score Conversion Chart

SCALED SCORE	RAW SCORE (Number Correct)			
Estimated ACT Score	Test 1 English	Test 2 Math	Test 3 Reading	Test 4 Science
36	75	60	40	40
35	74	60	40	40
34	73	59	39	39
33	72	58	39	39
32	71	57	38	38
31	70	55-56	37	37
30	69	53-54	36	36
29	68	50-52	35	35
28	67	48-49	34	34
27	65-66	45-47	33	33
26	63-64	43-44	32	32
25	61-62	40-42	31	30-31
24	58-60	38-39	30	28-29
23	56-57	35-37	29	26-27
22	53-55	33-34	28	24-25
21	49-52	31-32	27	21-23
20	46-48	28-30	25-26	19-20
19	44-45	26-27	23-24	17-18
18	41-43	23-25	21-22	16
17	39-40	20-22	19-20	15
16	36-38	17-19	17-18	14
15	34-35	15-16	15-16	13
14	30-33	13-14	13-14	12
13	28-29	11-12	12-13	11
12	25-27	9-10	10-11	10
11	23-24	8	9	9
10	20-22	7	8	8
9	17-19	6	7	7
8	14-16	5	6	6
7	12-13	4	5	5
6	9-11	3	4	4
5	7-8	2	3	3
4	4-6	1	2	2
3	3	1	1	1
2	2	0	0	0
1	1	0	0	0

Progress Chart

Test 1		Test 2		Test 3		Test 4		Test 5	
English Total Number Missed:	ACT Score:	English Total Number Missed:	ACT Score:	English Total Number Missed:	ACT Score:	English Total Number Missed:	ACT Score:	English Total Number Missed:	ACT Score:
Math Total Number Missed:	ACT Score:	Math Total Number Missed:	ACT Score:	Math Total Number Missed:	ACT Score:	Math Total Number Missed:	ACT Score:	Math Total Number Missed:	ACT Score:
Reading Total Number Missed:	ACT Score:	Reading Total Number Missed:	ACT Score:	Reading Total Number Missed:	ACT Score:	Reading Total Number Missed:	ACT Score:	Reading Total Number Missed:	ACT Score:
Science Total Number Missed:	ACT Score:	Science Total Number Missed:	ACT Score:	Science Total Number Missed:	ACT Score:	Science Total Number Missed:	ACT Score:	Science Total Number Missed:	ACT Score:
Composite Score:		**Composite Score:**		**Composite Score:**		**Composite Score:**		**Composite Score:**	

About this Course

Why are you taking the ACT? You are taking it to get into college, and possibly to win some scholarships. How do you get into college and win scholarships?

Getting the most number of ACT questions right demonstrates your knowledge to college admission boards and financial aid organizations. You demonstrate your knowledge by getting the most number of ACT test questions right. That is your goal for this course: TO GET THE MOST NUMBER OF QUESTIONS RIGHT.

Your goal is NOT to get all of the questions right. Why? Because if you spend too much time on a difficult or impossible question, even though you may find the correct answer to that ONE question, you run out of time to thoroughly answer many more easy questions. You have not gotten the *most* number of questions right, and you have not shown what you know.

In this course, you will learn to identify and answer the easy questions first, then solve or guess intelligently on the difficult questions. If you apply the following ten tactics on all four sections of the ACT, you will GET THE MOST NUMBER OF QUESTIONS RIGHT.

Quick Facts

- The ACT is about three hours long (three and a half with the Writing test).
- There will be a short break between the second and third subject tests.
- The exam is composed of four subject tests and an optional Writing test.

    English (45 minutes, 75 questions)
    Math (60 minutes, 60 questions)
    Reading (35 minute, 40 questions)
    Science (35 minutes, 40 questions)
    Writing (30 minutes, 1 essay question)

All About the ACT

What is the ACT?

The ACT is an exam taken by high school juniors and seniors for admission into college. It is not an IQ test; it's a test of problem-solving skills – which means you can improve your performance by preparing for it.

The ACT consists of four subject tests: English, Math, Reading, and Science, as well as the optional Writing test. All the subject tests are primarily designed to test skills rather than knowledge, though some knowledge is required – particularly in English, for which a familiarity with grammar and writing mechanics is

important, and in Math, for which you need to know the basic math concepts taught in a regular high school curriculum. The Writing test tests your ability to communicate clearly your position on an issue.

How the ACT is Scored

ACT scaled scores range from 1 to 36. Nearly half of all test takers score within a much narrower range: 17-23. Tests at different dates vary slightly, but the following data are based on a recent administration of the test and can be considered typical.

ACT Approximate Percentile Rank*	Scaled (or Composite) Score	Percentage of Questions Correct
99%	31	90%
90%	26	75%
76%	23	63%
54%	20	53%
28%	17	43%

*Percentage of ACT takers scoring at or below given score

The ACT Scores You Will Get

Here is the full battery of ACT scores (1-36) you will receive. Few people will care about anything except your composite score for college admissions, though some schools use the highest individual subject scores for course placement or to form super score.

English Score (1-36)	Usage/Mechanics subscore (1-18); Rhetorical Skills subscore (1-18); (Optional) Writing subscore (2-12)
Math Score (1-36)	Prealgebra/Elementary Algebra subscore (1-18); Algebra/Coordinate Geometry subscore (1-18); Plane Geometry/Trigonometry subscore (1-18)
Reading Score (1-36)	Social Sciences/Sciences subscore (1-18); Arts/Literature subscore (1-18)
Science Score (1-36)	There are no subscores in Science.
(Optional) Combined English-Writing Score (1-36)	Does not count towards your composite score, but colleges will see it.

The Composite Score

The most important score for most test takers is the composite score, which is an average of the four major subject scores. This is the score used by most colleges and universities in the admissions process. Use the scoring chart at the end of this chapter to determine your subject and composite scores on practice tests.

The Optional Writing Test

You should decide whether to take the ACT Writing test based on the admissions policies of the schools to which you will apply and on the advice of your high school guidance counselors. A list of colleges requiring the Writing test is maintained on the ACT website (www.act.org/aap/writing).

Summary of the ACT

1. The ACT consists of four required subject tests (English, Math, Reading, and Science) plus an optional Writing test.
2. Total testing time is about three hours, plus half an hour for the Writing test.
3. All questions are multiple choice except on the Writing test which is one essay question.
4. There is **no** penalty for a wrong answer so you should always guess.
5. ACT composite scores range from 1-36.

General Tactics for the ACT Test

If you apply the following ten tactics on all four sections of the ACT, you will get the most number of questions right.

Tactic 1: Two- Pass Method (DIE)

Read the question and ask yourself: Is this question easy, difficult, or impossible? The answer is subjective. You get to decide which questions are easy, difficult, or impossible for you.

If you judge it impossible, quickly guess and move on. Choose a letter such as C or H and stick with it throughout the test.

If it is difficult, circle the question and come back to it on the second pass.

If it is easy, answer it on the first pass.

Example

If sec2x = 4, which of the following could be sin x?
- A. 1.73205
- B. 3.14159
- C. $\sqrt{3}$
- D. $\dfrac{\sqrt{3}}{2}$
- E. Cannot be determined from the given information.

If you judge this question to be impossible, choose an answer such as C/H and move on. You may be thinking, "I can answer this in just a few minutes." But a few minutes are too many minutes when you only have one minute per question. Circle it as difficult and come back to it on the second pass.

Tactic 2: Stay within the time allowed for each subject test and for each passage.

You will not be allowed to take an iPhone into the test center. Locate a watch during this course and the actual ACT. Become familiar now with using a watch to keep track of your time.

Memorize the amount of time allowed for each subject test: 45 minutes for English, 60 minutes for Math, 35 minutes for Reading, and 35 minutes for Science.

Memorize the amount of time for each *passage* within each test: 8 minutes for each Reading passage, 9 minutes for each English passage, and five minutes for each Science passage, and an average of 1 minute for each Math question. Stay within these times. Do not borrow time from the next passage.

Use ALL of the time. If you have more than one minute left per test, you are moving too quickly. Slow down and work carefully.

Tactic 3: Slash the bubbles.
Don't waste precious time tediously filling in each bubble as you go. Instead, make a quick slash in the correct answer bubble and move on to the next question.

Reserve about a minute at the end of each subject test or at the end of each passage to fill in the bubbles. You will be amazed at how much time you save. Be sure to do this as you practice so you become comfortable with the tactic. Use the answer sheets provided on the practice tests. Do not mark the answers in the test book.

Tactic 4: Stay on the grid.
Most of us have had that horrible experience of realizing, usually with only seconds left to finish the test, that we unknowingly got off the answer grid and our answers do not match the grid. Avoid

unnecessarily losing points by using the edge of a paper to guide you on the grid. Check the grid with the answer sheet after every passage or after every 5 to 10 questions.

Tactic 5: Use the Q. S. NRAF plan.

Read the **Questions**. **Skim** the passage. As you read, **Note** where answers to questions are found in the passage. **Refer** back to the passage when answering questions. **Answer** the question in your own words, and then **Find** the answer choice that best fits.

Often to find the correct answer, you won't need to know or understand all the information in the passage. You only need to know what is required to answer the questions. There may be 100 facts, but you only need to know 10 facts to answer the 10 questions.

To save time and get the most number right, here is what QSNRAF looks like: Read the **questions** first, underlining key words and phrases. DO NOT look at the answer choices at this point.

Next, **skim** the passage. When you come across information related to one of the questions, **note** it by underlining, writing in the margin, or drawing pictures.

Now, read the first question again. **Refer** back to the relevant portion of the passage, and **answer** the question in your own words.

Finally, **find** the matching answer among the choices and slash the bubble.

Example

"Isaac Newton was born in 1642 in the hamlet of Woolsthorpe in Lincolnshire, England. But he is more famous as a man of Cambridge, where he studied and taught..."

Now cover the above passage and try to answer the question. No looking!

Which of the following does the author imply is a fact about Newton's birth?

   A. It occurred in Lincoln, a small hamlet in England.

      Yes! Something was said about Lincoln. This must be the correct answer.

   B. It took place in a part of England known for raising sheep.

      I read something about sheep and wool. Yep, B is correct.

   C. It caused Newton to seek his education at Cambridge.

      Now I remember, the passage did mention Cambridge. But how can they all be right?

   D. It did not occur in a large metropolitan setting.

      The word "metropolitan" wasn't mentioned, was it?

When you uncover the passage, the correct answer quickly becomes clear. Newton was born in Lincolnshire, not Lincoln. Therefore, A is not correct. The name of the hamlet of his birth was Woolsthorpe; no mention of sheep. B is not correct. He "is more famous as a man of Cambridge", but the question asked about his birth. Nothing is stated or implied about his birth causing this. Therefore, C is not correct. That leaves D, "It did not occur in a large metropolitan setting." Nothing is specifically stated about the size of his birthplace, but if you know that hamlet means a very small village, or the suffix "et" means "little", and you know that "metropolitan" refers to a large metropolis, or populated area, then you can look for the answer in a different format. Therefore, D is the correct answer. If you try to remember the facts without referring back to the passage, you might easily confuse the facts.

Tactic 6: Eliminate and guess.

Answer every question on the test. There is no penalty for incorrect answers. If you leave a question unanswered, there is a 100% chance you will get it wrong.

Even if you guess randomly, there is a 25% chance you will get it right.

If you ask, "Which of these answer choices is probably NOT the

Tactics 6 through 10 will primarily be used to answer difficult questions on the second pass.

correct answer?" and are able to eliminate two, you have a 50% chance of getting it correct.

If you can narrow the answer choices to two options, ask yourself, "Which of the two answers is most probably correct?"

Tactic 7: Answer the question being asked.

Example

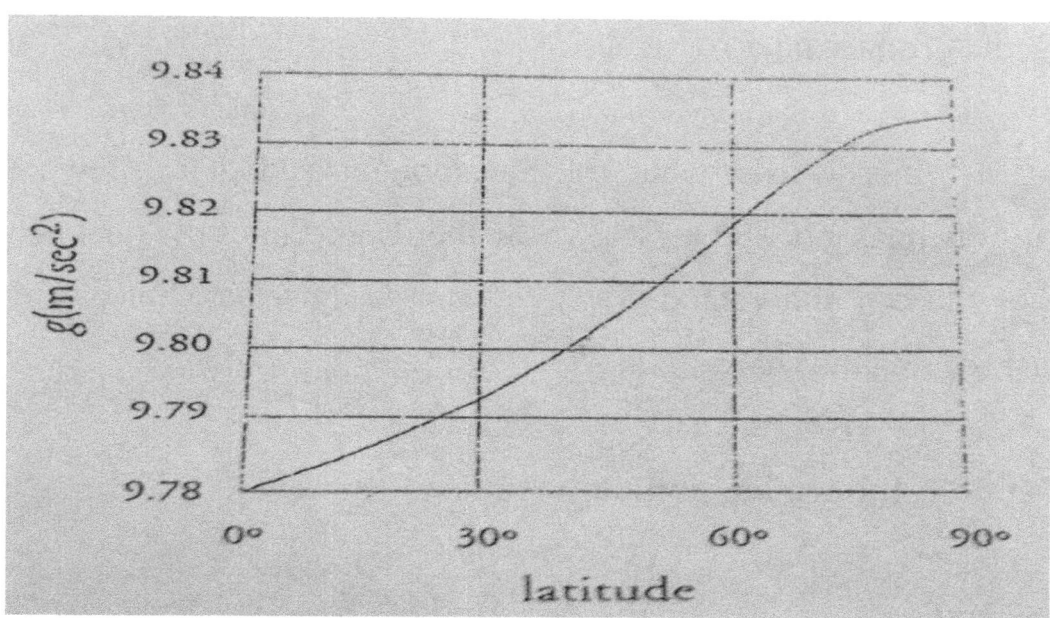

According to Figure 1, at approximately what latitude would calculations using an estimated value at sea level of g = 9.80 m/sec² produce the least error?

  A. 0°
  B. 15°

C. 40°

D. 60°

At what latitude would the calculations using a value of g = 9.80 m/sec² produce the least error? What does that mean?

Ask yourself, "Where would an estimate for g of 9.80 m/sec² produce the least error?" It would be a latitude where 9.80 m/sec² is the real value of g. If you find the latitude at which the real value of g is 9.80 m/sec², then using 9.80 m/sec² as an estimate there would produce no error at all.

So, in other words, what this question is asking is: At what latitude does g = 9.80 m/sec²? Now that is a form of the question that you can understand. Now, you can easily select choice C by just reading the chart.

Tactic 8: Ignore insignificant issues.

Example

"... China was certainly one of the cradles of civilization. It's obvious that, China has a long history. As is the case with other ancient cultures, the early history of China is lost in mythology... "

F. NO CHANGE

G. It's obvious that China has a long history.

H. Obviously; China has a long history.

J. OMIT the underlined portion.

In this question, the test makers are counting on you to waste time worrying about punctuation. Does that comma belong? Can you use a semicolon here? These issues might be worrisome, but there's a bigger issue here: Does the sentence belong in the passage at all? No, it does not. If China has an ancient culture and was a cradle of civilization, it must have a long history. Redundancy is the relevant issue here, not punctuation. Choice J is correct. Ignore the insignificant issues; zoom out and look for the glaring problem.

Tactic 9: Look for the correct answer in a different form.
Do not choose an answer choice simply because the terms are the same as those used in the passage. The passage may have used the word *fortress,* but the correct answer may use the synonym *citadel.* The question might entirely use *decimals,* and the correct answer choice be presented in *fractions.*

Tactic 10: Put the question in an understandable format.
Restate the question in your own words. Ask yourself, "What is being asked here?"

Example

Jason bought a painting with a frame 1 inch wide. If the dimensions of the outside of the frame are 5 inches by 7 inches, which of the following could be the length of one of the sides of the painting inside the frame?

　　E. 3 inches
　　F. 4 inches
　　G. 5 ½ inches
　　H. 6 ½ inches
　　I. 7 inches

Just looking at the question for the first time, you might be tempted simply to subtract 1 from the outside dimensions and think that the inside dimensions are 4 by 6 (and pick G). Why is this not correct? Because the frame goes all the way around – both above and below the painting, both to the right and to the left. This would have been clear if you had put the problem in a form you could understand and use.

For instance, you might have made the situation graphic by actually sketching out the painting frame.

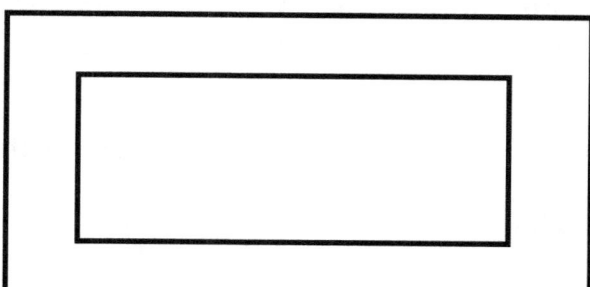

When you draw the picture frame like this, you realize that if the outside dimensions are 5 by 7, the inside dimensions must be 3 by 5. Thus, the correct answer is F.

So remember: On the ACT, you have to put everything into a form that you can understand and use.

Troubleshooting General Tactics

Since your goal is to get the most number of questions right, you will log the questions you most often miss. We will use this information to strengthen you in your weak areas so you can get similar questions right next time.

To complete the chart, find where the tactic and the subject intersect and write the question number in that box. Answer the question:
"I missed this problem because I did NOT..."

Tactics	English	Math	Reading	Science	Total missed for this reason
1. Do the two-pass method • Make two passes • Limit my time on difficult or impossible questions					
2. Stay within time • Use all of my time • Finish in time and had to guess					
3. Slash bubbles					
4. Stay on the grid					
5. Remember Q. S. NRAF/steps • Do one or more of the steps					
6. Eliminate and guess • Fill in the bubble • Eliminated one or more answer choices, but guessed the wrong answer • I guessed incorrectly on an impossible question					
7. Answer the question being asked • Understand the meaning of certain words • Understand the question • Understand what was being asked for					
8. Ignore insignificant issues					
9. Look for correct answer in different form					
10. Put question in an understandable format					

Troubleshooting General Tactics

Since your goal is to get the most number of questions right, you will log the questions you most often miss. We will use this information to strengthen you in your weak areas so you can get similar questions right next time.

To complete the chart, find where the tactic and the subject intersect and write the question number in that box. Answer the question:

"I missed this problem because I did NOT…"

Tactics	English	Math	Reading	Science	Total missed for this reason
1. Do the two-pass method • Make two passes • Limit my time on difficult or impossible questions					
2. Stay within time • Use all of my time • Finish in time and had to guess					
3. Slash bubbles					
4. Stay on the grid					
5. Remember Q. S. NRAF/steps • Do one or more of the steps					
6. Eliminate and guess • Fill in the bubble • Eliminated one or more answer choices, but guessed the wrong answer • I guessed incorrectly on an impossible question					
7. Answer the question being asked • Understand the meaning of certain words • Understand the question • Understand what was being asked for					
8. Ignore insignificant issues					
9. Look for correct answer in different form					
10. Put question in an understandable format					

Troubleshooting General Tactics

Since your goal is to get the most number of questions right, you will log the questions you most often miss. We will use this information to strengthen you in your weak areas so you can get similar questions right next time.

To complete the chart, find where the tactic and the subject intersect and write the question number in that box. Answer the question:
"I missed this problem because I did NOT…"

Tactics	English	Math	Reading	Science	Total missed for this reason
1. Do the two-pass method • Make two passes • Limit my time on difficult or impossible questions					
2. Stay within time • Use all of my time • Finish in time and had to guess					
3. Slash bubbles					
4. Stay on the grid					
5. Remember Q. S. NRAF/steps • Do one or more of the steps					
6. Eliminate and guess • Fill in the bubble • Eliminated one or more answer choices, but guessed the wrong answer • I guessed incorrectly on an impossible question					
7. Answer the question being asked • Understand the meaning of certain words • Understand the question • Understand what was being asked for					
8. Ignore insignificant issues					
9. Look for correct answer in different form					
10. Put question in an understandable format					

Troubleshooting General Tactics

Since your goal is to get the most number of questions right, you will log the questions you most often miss. We will use this information to strengthen you in your weak areas so you can get similar questions right next time.

To complete the chart, find where the tactic and the subject intersect and write the question number in that box. Answer the question:
"I missed this problem because I did NOT…"

Tactics	English	Math	Reading	Science	Total missed for this reason
1. Do the two-pass method • Make two passes • Limit my time on difficult or impossible questions					
2. Stay within time • Use all of my time • Finish in time and had to guess					
3. Slash bubbles					
4. Stay on the grid					
5. Remember Q. S. NRAF/steps • Do one or more of the steps					
6. Eliminate and guess • Fill in the bubble • Eliminated one or more answer choices, but guessed the wrong answer • I guessed incorrectly on an impossible question					
7. Answer the question being asked • Understand the meaning of certain words • Understand the question • Understand what was being asked for					
8. Ignore insignificant issues					
9. Look for correct answer in different form					
10. Put question in an understandable format					

Troubleshooting General Tactics

Since your goal is to get the most number of questions right, you will log the questions you most often miss. We will use this information to strengthen you in your weak areas so you can get similar questions right next time.

To complete the chart, find where the tactic and the subject intersect and write the question number in that box. Answer the question:
"**I missed this problem because I did NOT…**"

Tactics	English	Math	Reading	Science	Total missed for this reason
1. Do the two-pass method • Make two passes • Limit my time on difficult or impossible questions					
2. Stay within time • Use all of my time • Finish in time and had to guess					
3. Slash bubbles					
4. Stay on the grid					
5. Remember Q. S. NRAF/steps • Do one or more of the steps					
6. Eliminate and guess • Fill in the bubble • Eliminated one or more answer choices, but guessed the wrong answer • I guessed incorrectly on an impossible question					
7. Answer the question being asked • Understand the meaning of certain words • Understand the question • Understand what was being asked for					
8. Ignore insignificant issues					
9. Look for correct answer in different form					
10. Put question in an understandable format					

Quick Facts

• The Reading Test is 35 minutes long.

• There are four passages with 10 questions each. Plan 8 minutes for each passage and set of questions.

• Passage Content: There will be one passage on each of the following subject areas:
- Prose Fiction
- Social Science
- Humanities
- Natural Science

• The questions do NOT get progressively more difficult.

• Read the directions now so you do not need to take time to read them again during the test.

> Directions: *There are several passages in this test. Each passage is accompanied by several questions. After reading a passage, choose the best answer to each question and fill in the corresponding oval on your answer document. You may refer to the passages as often as necessary.*

Types of Reading Questions

In each passage, there will be three types of questions.

1. **Specific detail**

Questions are asked about matters specifically stated in the passage. For example, "What color was her dress?" The answer however may be worded one way in the passage (red), and another way in the answer (scarlet).

2. Inference

The answer is not specifically stated in the passage. You must read between the lines. For example, you ask, "Are you going to the football game?" I answer, "I love football." I have not specifically answered your question, but you can read between the lines. It is more likely than not that I am going to the football game.

3. Big picture

These are questions about *main ideas*, *themes*, *moods*, *tones*, *structure*, *point of view*, and other literary concepts. They often address the passage as a whole.

Tactics for Understanding the Reading Test
1. Timing

You will have 35 minutes for 40 questions. There are four passages and each passage has a set of 10 questions. Think of the Reading Test as 4 separate tests, each 8 minutes long. You cannot borrow time from one test to another. Spend 5 or 6 minutes on each passage during the first pass and 2 or 3 minutes on the second pass.

2. Apply Q. S. NRAF

Read the **Questions**. **Skim** the passage. As you read, **Note** where answers to questions are found in the passage. **Refer** back to the passage when answering questions. **Answer** the question in your own words, and then **Find** the answer choice that best fits.

Begin with reading only the **questions**. DO NOT read the answer choices yet. As you read, underline key words in the questions. The following are always key words:
- References to lines or paragraphs,
- Direct quotes,
- The word *except* or *not* when used in a question asking which of the answer choices does not apply,
- Words such as *infer, suggest,* and *intend* alert you that this may be an inference question,
- Literary terms such as *main purpose, main function, main idea,* and *point of view*.

Skim the passage. Read for two purposes only: 1) to gain a general idea of the passage content, 2) to locate key words or content to answer the 10 questions. Do not attempt to understand every detail of the passage.

Note in the passage where answers to the questions are found. Do this by underlining, circling, making notes or drawing pictures in the margin. You are not looking for the answer yet, only where the

answer is found in the passage.

Do NOT try to remember or comprehend all the facts and details of the passage. Even if you could read, comprehend, and answer all the questions in 8 minutes, you only need enough information to answer the 10 questions.

Read the question again and ask yourself: Is this question easy, difficult, or impossible? The answer is subjective. You get to decide which questions are easy, difficult, or impossible for you.

If the question is impossible, quickly eliminate and guess, or just guess, slash the bubble, and move on.

If the question is easy, answer it now. Refer back to the passage, put the answer in your own words, find that answer among the answer choices, and slash the bubble.

If the question is difficult, circle the question number and return to it during the second pass. Questions that ask about the passage as a whole (big picture) should always be answered on the second pass. Clues to these types of questions are words and phrases such as *main purpose*, *in the context of the passage*, and *point of view*. At that time, employ general tactics such as answer the question being asked, ignore insignificant issues, look for the answer in a different format, or put the question in an

understandable form.

3. If you come across an unfamiliar word, guess the meaning from the context or from the root word

4. Special tactics for the prose/fiction passage

Pay attention to the characters of the passage. There will probably be questions about them.

Zoom out and get in big picture and inference mind set. Read between the lines. Look for *themes*, *tones*, and *moods*. You may also be asked to evaluate the writing.

5. If you are running out of time

Skip reading the passage and answer the questions by looking at the passage.

Read the first and last paragraph or the first and last sentence of each paragraph. The topic or theme of a particular passage can be found in the first and last paragraph of that passage. The theme of a particular paragraph can be found in the first or last sentence of every paragraph.

Spend 11 minutes, rather than 8 minutes on three passages and skip reading the 4th passage. Spend one or two minutes filling in the same letter – such as *C/H* – for the answers for the 4th passage.

6. If one type of passage is obviously more difficult for you, do that type of passage first.

Or if you decide to employ the previous tactic, apply it to the most difficult type of passage.

Application of Reading Tactics

Work through the following Reading passage and 10 questions. Apply the tactics you just learned. Do not time yourself, but take as much time as you need to understand how the tactics apply.

Humanities: This passage is adapted from the article "Finding Philosophy" by Colin McGinn (©2003 by Prospect)

Descartes (line 63) refers to René Descartes (1596-1650), a French mathematician, philosopher, and scientist.

I have been an academic philosopher for the past 30 years. I came from an academically disinclined background in the northeast of England, my relatives being mainly coalminers and other manual workers. I was the first in my family to attend university, and indeed had no thought of it until age 17, when a teacher mentioned it at school. My father had become a successful builder, so we were not materially deprived, and it was expected that I would become a sort of technical worker. The idea that I might one day become a professional philosopher was inconceivable in those days, to me and everyone else. I was simply not living in a place where that kind of thing ever happened; it was far likelier – though still not likely at all – that I would become a pop star (I played drums in a rock band).

The paperback British edition of my memoir "The Making of a Philosopher" has a photograph on the cover of a man sitting on a bench, placed in a grey and listless landscape. He is overlooking the sea on a misty grim day, and the atmosphere is bleak and melancholy. The man, hunched up, immobile, coiled almost, has a pensive posture, as if frozen in thought. This picture is based on a story I tell in the book about sitting on a bench in Blackpool, aged 18, pondering the metaphysical question of how objects relate to their properties. Is an object just the sum total of its properties, a mere coalescence of general features, or does it somehow lie behind its properties, supporting them, a solid peg on which they happen to hang? When I look at an object, do I really see the object itself, or just the appearance its properties offer to me? I remember the feeling of fixation that came over me when I thought about these questions – a kind of floating fascination, a still perplexity.

When I look back on this period in my late teens, I recall the harnessing of undirected mental energy by intellectual pursuits. Up until then, my mental energy had gone into things like reading "Melody Maker", which contained fairly serious articles of pop musicians; I always knew the top 20 off by heart, and studied the articles about drummers intensely, hoping to improve my own technique. I suspect that this kind of swashing mental energy is fairly typical of boys that age. School doesn't seem to connect with it, and it goes off in search of some object of interest, often trivial, sometimes destructive. In my case, it was philosophy that seized that energy and converted it into a passion – though one that took several years to form fully. It is a delicate and fastidious energy that I am speaking of, despite its power, and it will only be satisfied by certain employments, which of course vary

from person to person. I had had a similar passion from chemistry when I was ten, and for butterflies and lizards before that. *How to harness such passions to formal education remains a great and unresolved problem.*

It was – of course – a teacher who tapped into my formless and fizzing mental energy. Mr. Marsh, a teacher of divinity, brimmingly Christian, a man with very active eyebrows and sharp enunciation, in love with scholarship (oh, how he relished that word) – it was he who first brought out my inner philosopher. From him I heard of Descartes, locked up in his room, wondering whether anything could really be known beyond his own existence. But what I mainly got from the enthusiastic Mr. Marsh was the desire to study. His own passion to study shown through, and he managed to make it seem, if not glamorous, then at least exhilarating – when done the right way and in the right spirit. Pencils and stationary were made to seem like shiny tools, and the pleasure of making one's mark on a blank sheet of paper hymned. Choosing a good spot to study was emphasized. Above all, I learned a very valuable lesson, one that had hitherto escaped me: make notes. Thinking and writing should be indissoluble activities, the hand ministering to the thought, the thought shaped by the hand. Today, if I find myself without pen and paper and thoughts start to arrive, my fingers begin to twitch and I long for those implements of cogitation. *With such rudimentary tools you can perform the miracle of turning an invisible thought into a concrete mark, bringing the ethereal interior into the public external world, refining it into something precious and permanent.* The physical pleasure of writing, which I find survives in the use of a computer, is something worth dwelling on in matters of education.

1. The passage is best described as being told from the point of view of a philosopher who is:
A. discussing metaphysical questions that have troubled philosophers since the time of Descartes.
B. presenting in chronological order the key events in his thirty-year professional career.
C. reflecting on his own early, developing interest in philosophy and in scholarship generally.
D. advising professional educators on how to get more students to study philosophy.

2. Based on the passage, which of the following was most likely the first to engage the author's passionate interest?
F. Drumming
G. Philosophy
H. Chemistry
J. Butterflies

3. The main purpose of the last paragraph is to:
A. reveal the enduring impact of Mr. Marsh's lessons on the author.

B. acknowledge that the author came to doubt some of Mr. Marsh's teachings.
C. describe a typical class as taught by Mr. Marsh.
D. present a biographical sketch of Mr. Marsh.

4. The passage indicates that the man in the book-cover photograph represents:
F. Descartes, wondering what could be known.
G. Mr. Marsh, deep in scholarly thought.
H. the author at age seventeen, thinking about enrolling in college.
J. the author at age eighteen, contemplating a philosophical issue.

5. The author mentions *Melody Maker*, the top 20, and articles about musicians primarily to suggest that his:
A. early interest in music has remained with him to the present.
B. time spent playing music should instead have been spent reading.
C. fascination with pop music and musicians gave focus to his life for a time.
D. commitment to study enabled him to perfect his drumming technique.

6. In the third paragraph, the author most nearly characterizes the energy he refers to as:
F. potent yet difficult to channel in a constructive way.
G. powerful and typically leading to destructive results.
H. delicate and inevitably wasted in trivial undertakings.
J. gentle yet capable of uniting people who have different interests.

7. Viewed in the context of the passage, the statement in lines 55-56 (italicized in the third paragraph) is most likely intended to suggest that:
A. schools should require students to take philosophy courses.
B. students can become passionate when learning about science in school.
C. schools need to keep searching for ways to tap into students' deeply held interests.
D. students should resolve to take school courses that interest them.

8. The author calls pen and paper "rudimentary tools" (bolded in the fourth paragraph) as part of his argument that:
F. the use of computers has made the use of pen and paper obsolete.
G. students should become skilled with pen and paper before moving on to better tools.
H. while writing in pen and paper can be pleasant, it can also be physically painful.
J. although seemingly simple, pen and paper allow people to perform great feats.

9. In the context of the passage, lines 17-23 (italicized in the second paragraph) are best described as presenting images of:
A. gloom, tension, and fascination.
B. anger, bitterness, and betrayal.
C. stillness, peacefulness, and relaxation.

D. frustration, surprise, and satisfaction.

10. Which of the following does NOT reasonably describe the transition the author presents in lines 80-84 (italicized in the fourth paragraph)?
F. Precious to commonplace
G. Fleeting to permanent
H. Invisible to visible
J. Private to public

Answers: 1 – C; 2 – J; 3 – A; 4 – J; 5 – C; 6 – F; 7 – C; 8 – J; 9 – A; 10 - F

Troubleshooting Reading Tactics

For each question you missed, find the reason in the left column and write the question number in the adjacent right column.

Time? *I did not:*	Question Number	The Question? *I did not:*	Question Number	The Answer? *I did not:*	Question Number
• Spend 8 minutes on each passage		• Read the question first and underline key words		• See the answer when I skimmed the passage	
• Use all of my time		• Note where the answer is found in the passage		• Recognize the answer was in a different format from the question	
• Make two passes		• Refer back to the passage before I answered		• Guess the right answer	
• Identify the difficult or impossible questions, or I spent too much time on them during the first pass		• Put the question in my own words before selecting an answer		• Recognize insignificant issues in the answer choices	
• Slash the bubbles		• Understand the question		• Understand the meaning of important words	
• Stay on the grid		• Answer what was being asked			

For each question missed, record the level of difficulty, subject content, and question type. Write the question number in each of the three categories.

Degree			Content				Type		
Easy	Difficult	Impossible	Prose/Fiction	Social Science	Humanities	Natural Science	Specific Detail	Inference	Big Picture

Troubleshooting Reading Tactics

For each question you missed, find the reason in the left column and write the question number in the adjacent right column.

Time? *I did not:*	Question Number	The Question? *I did not:*	Question Number	The Answer? *I did not:*	Question Number
• Spend 8 minutes on each passage		• Read the question first and underline key words		• See the answer when I skimmed the passage	
• Use all of my time		• Note where the answer is found in the passage		• Recognize the answer was in a different format from the question	
• Make two passes		• Refer back to the passage before I answered		• Guess the right answer	
• Identify the difficult or impossible questions, or I spent too much time on them during the first pass		• Put the question in my own words before selecting an answer		• Recognize insignificant issues in the answer choices	
• Slash the bubbles		• Understand the question		• Understand the meaning of important words	
• Stay on the grid		• Answer what was being asked			

For each question missed, record the level of difficulty, subject content, and question type. Write the question number in each of the three categories.

Degree			Content				Type		
Easy	Difficult	Impossible	Prose/Fiction	Social Science	Humanities	Natural Science	Specific Detail	Inference	Big Picture

Troubleshooting Reading Tactics

For each question you missed, find the reason in the left column and write the question number in the adjacent right column.

Time? *I did not:*	Question Number	The Question? *I did not:*	Question Number	The Answer? *I did not:*	Question Number
• Spend 8 minutes on each passage		• Read the question first and underline key words		• See the answer when I skimmed the passage	
• Use all of my time		• Note where the answer is found in the passage		• Recognize the answer was in a different format from the question	
• Make two passes		• Refer back to the passage before I answered		• Guess the right answer	
• Identify the difficult or impossible questions, or I spent too much time on them during the first pass		• Put the question in my own words before selecting an answer		• Recognize insignificant issues in the answer choices	
• Slash the bubbles		• Understand the question		• Understand the meaning of important words	
• Stay on the grid		• Answer what was being asked			

For each question missed, record the level of difficulty, subject content, and question type. Write the question number in each of the three categories.

Degree			Content				Type		
Easy	Difficult	Impossible	Prose/Fiction	Social Science	Humanities	Natural Science	Specific Detail	Inference	Big Picture

Troubleshooting Reading Tactics

For each question you missed, find the reason in the left column and write the question number in the adjacent right column.

Time? *I did not:*	Question Number	The Question? *I did not:*	Question Number	The Answer? *I did not:*	Question Number
• Spend 8 minutes on each passage		• Read the question first and underline key words		• See the answer when I skimmed the passage	
• Use all of my time		• Note where the answer is found in the passage		• Recognize the answer was in a different format from the question	
• Make two passes		• Refer back to the passage before I answered		• Guess the right answer	
• Identify the difficult or impossible questions, or I spent too much time on them during the first pass		• Put the question in my own words before selecting an answer		• Recognize insignificant issues in the answer choices	
• Slash the bubbles		• Understand the question		• Understand the meaning of important words	
• Stay on the grid		• Answer what was being asked			

For each question missed, record the level of difficulty, subject content, and question type. Write the question number in each of the three categories.

Degree			Content				Type		
Easy	Difficult	Impossible	Prose/Fiction	Social Science	Humanities	Natural Science	Specific Detail	Inference	Big Picture

Troubleshooting Reading Tactics

For each question you missed, find the reason in the left column and write the question number in the adjacent right column.

Time? *I did not:*	Question Number	The Question? *I did not:*	Question Number	The Answer? *I did not:*	Question Number
• Spend 8 minutes on each passage		• Read the question first and underline key words		• See the answer when I skimmed the passage	
• Use all of my time		• Note where the answer is found in the passage		• Recognize the answer was in a different format from the question	
• Make two passes		• Refer back to the passage before I answered		• Guess the right answer	
• Identify the difficult or impossible questions, or I spent too much time on them during the first pass		• Put the question in my own words before selecting an answer		• Recognize insignificant issues in the answer choices	
• Slash the bubbles		• Understand the question		• Understand the meaning of important words	
• Stay on the grid		• Answer what was being asked			

For each question missed, record the level of difficulty, subject content, and question type. Write the question number in each of the three categories.

Degree			Content				Type		
Easy	Difficult	Impossible	Prose/Fiction	Social Science	Humanities	Natural Science	Specific Detail	Inference	Big Picture

Quick Facts

• There are 7 passages or sets of information and 40 questions total.

• The time allowed is 35 minutes. You will have 5 minutes per passage to complete 5 to 7 questions. Think of it as 7 five-minute test. Do not borrow time from one passage to another.

• The passages usually increase in difficulty.

• Calculators are not allowed on the Science test.

• Read the directions now so that you do not need to take time to read them again during the test.

> Directions: *There are several passages in this test. Each passage is followed by several questions. After reading the passage, choose the best answer to each question and fill in the corresponding oval on your answer document. You may refer to the passages as often as necessary. You are NOT permitted to use a calculator on this test.*

The Science Test Topics

On the ACT, you will find all high school science: physics, chemistry, biology, astronomy, geology, meteorology, environmental.

BUT all you need to know is provided in the test. This is more about reading graphs, charts and diagrams than knowing science!

Types of Passages and Questions

You will find three types of passages and questions in the Science test.

1. Experimental

There are 3 passages of this type with 6 questions each. There are a total of 18 experimental questions on the Science test. This is almost half of the Science questions. If your goal is to get the most number of questions right, you will want to master the experimental questions. The experimental format is presented in research summaries or descriptions of several related experiments.

2. Data Analysis

There are 2-3 passages with 5 questions each of this type. The total number of Data Analysis questions is 10-15, or one-fourth to one-third of the Science questions. Since you want to get the most number of questions right, Data Analysis questions should be your second focus.

You will recognize the data analysis format because the information is represented in graphs, tables, charts, and other schematic forms.

3. Conflicting Viewpoints/Principle

Conflicting Viewpoints/Principle passages consist of several related hypotheses or views that are inconsistent with one another. You will find one of these passages with 7 questions in each Science test.

Tactics for Understanding the Science Test
General Science Tactics

Do not rely on your own knowledge of science. All the information you need is given in the passage.

Being familiar with science vocabulary will be very helpful on the test. At the end of this section, you will find several pages of science vocabulary.

Read the first question. Ask yourself: Is it easy, difficult, or impossible?

Easy questions can be answered by referring back to the graphics. If the question is easy, answer it now. Refer back to the passage, put the answer in your own words, find that answer among the answer choices, and slash the bubble.

Difficult questions involve reading the written portion of the passage. Answer the difficult questions on the second pass by reading the written portion of the passage. If the question is impossible, quickly eliminate and guess, or just guess, and move on.

Tactics for Data Analysis Passages

Understand How to Read Graphics

The main purpose of all graphics is to show how facts relate to one another. Different graphics show different types of relationships. For example, a line graph shows how something changes over time, and a picture diagram shows how all the parts of something fit together. This section will help you read and understand the most common types of graphics.

Graphs

Graphs show how different pieces of information are related. The most common kinds of graphs are line graphs, pie graphs, and bar graphs.

Line Graph: *A line graph shows how things change over time.* It starts with an L-shaped grid. The horizontal line of the grid stands for passing time (seconds, minutes, years, centuries). The vertical line of the grid shows the subject of the graph. The line graph below shows the amounts of carbon monoxide emitted into the atmosphere in the years 1987 through 1996.

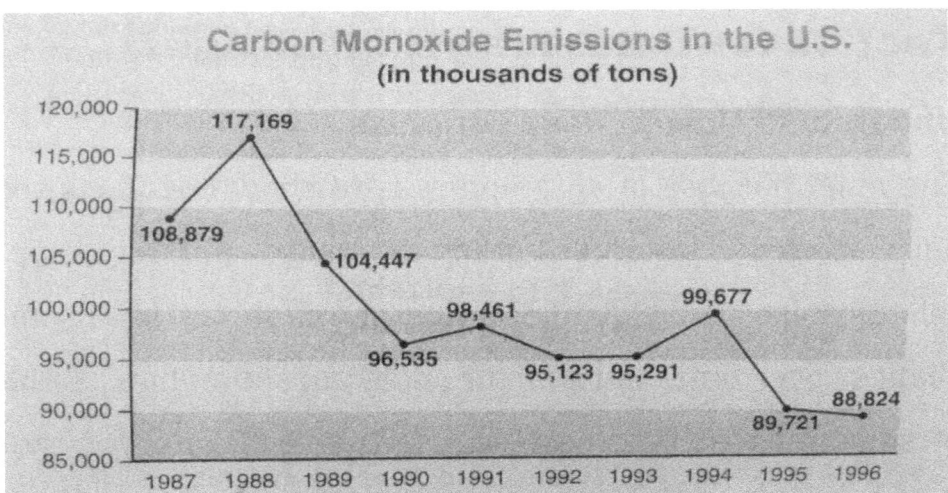

Pie Graph: *A pie graph shows proportions and how each proportion, or part, relates to the other parts as well as to the whole "pie."* The pie graph below shows the sources of carbon monoxide emissions in 1996, and what proportion of total emissions each source produced.

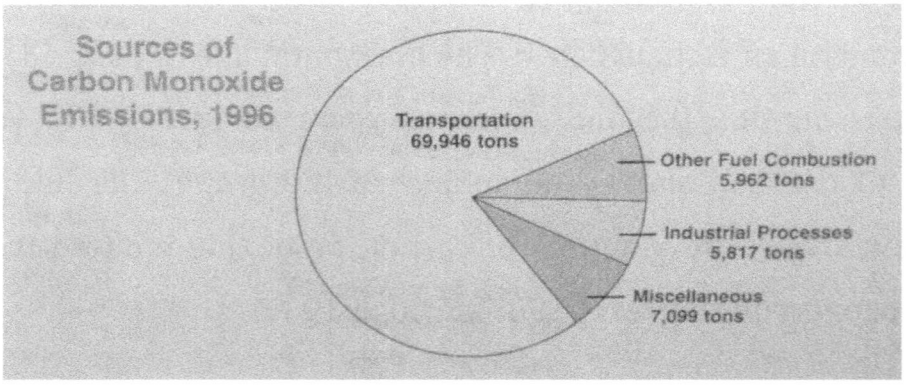

Bar Graph: A bar graph uses bars (sometimes called columns) to stand for the subjects of the graph. Unlike line graphs, bar graphs do not show how things change over time. Instead, like a snapshot, they *show how things compare*

at one point in time.

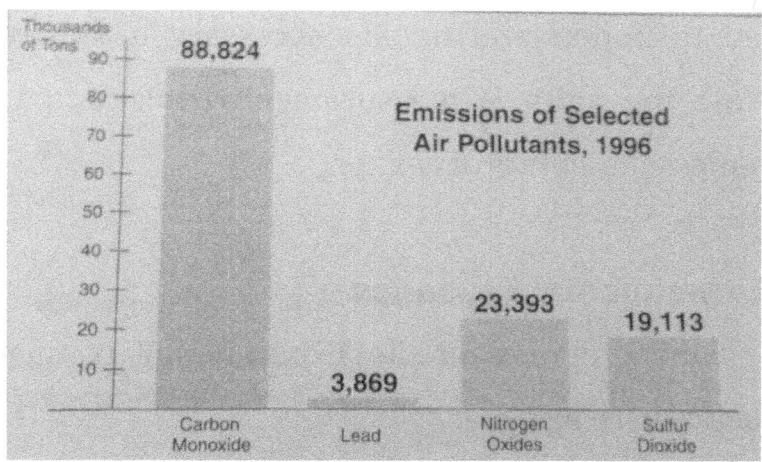

Stacked Bar Graph: A stacked bar graph is a special kind of bar graph that gives more detailed information than a regular bar graph. Besides comparing the bars, it *compares parts within the bars themselves.*

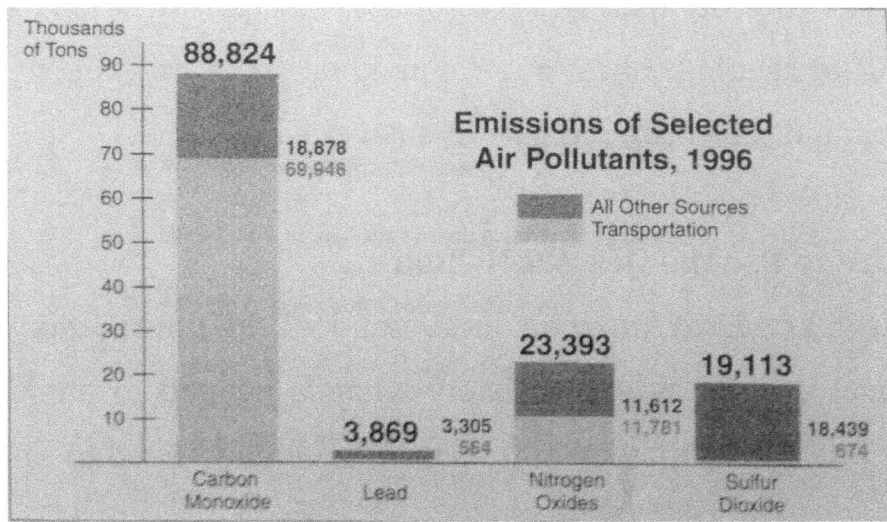

First, take a quick glance at the graphics. Ask yourself: What is being represented in the tables, graphs, or charts? What do the columns represent? What do the rows represent? At this point, you do not need to understand every detail of the graphics. You will only need to understand details necessary to answer the questions. Note the units of measurement. Look for patterns, changes, extremes, and points of change.

Tactics for Experimental Passages

You will see some graphics on the Experimental passages, so apply those tactics here also.

Pay attention to the control group and the variation group. Ask yourself: What factor is varied? What is the result or the difference between the two groups? Analyze the results.

Tactics for Conflicting Viewpoints/Principle Passages

Approach the Conflicting Viewpoints/Principle questions as you would a reading question. Remember, you do not need to understand the entire passage to answer a question.

Be Sure to Use the Q. S. NRAF Plan

You won't need to know or understand all the information in the passage. You only need to know what is needed to answer the questions. There may be 100 facts, but you only need to know 10 facts to answer the 10 questions.

Read the **Questions**. **Skim** the passage. As you read, **Note** where answers to questions are found in the passage. **Refer** back to the passage when answering questions. **Answer** the question in your own word. **Find** the answer choice that best fits.

To save time and get the most number right, read the questions first, underlining key words and phrases. DO NOT look at the answer choices at this point.

Next, skim the passage. When you come across information related to one of the questions, note it by underlining, writing in the margin, or drawing pictures. Spend most of your time reading and underlining. Ask yourself: Who, what, where, when, why, and how. Pay attention to conflicting viewpoints. Determine each scientist's view and identify the supporting and undermining evidence.

Now, read the first question again. Refer back to the relevant portion of the passage, and answer the question in your own words.

Finally, find the matching answer among the choices and slash the bubble.

Application of Science Tactics

Finch beak depth (see Figure 1) is an inheritable trait (it can be passed from parent to offspring).

Figure 1

Researchers studied the beak depth of 2 species of finches, *Geospiza fortis* and *Geospiza fuliginosa*. Both species live on Island A. *G. fortis* alone lives on Island B, and *G. fuliginosa* alone lives on Island C. For both species, the primary food is seeds. Birds with shallower beaks can efficiently crush and eat only small seeds. Birds with deeper beaks can crush and eat both large and small seeds, but they prefer small seeds.

Study 1

Researchers captured 100 *G. fortis* finches and 100 *G. fuliginsosa* finches on Island A. They tagged each bird, measured its beak depth, and released it. Then they calculated the percent of birds having each of the beak depths that had been measured. The researchers followed the same procedures with 100 *G. fortis* finches from Island B and 100 *G. fuliginosa* finches from Island C. The results of this study are shown in Figure 2.

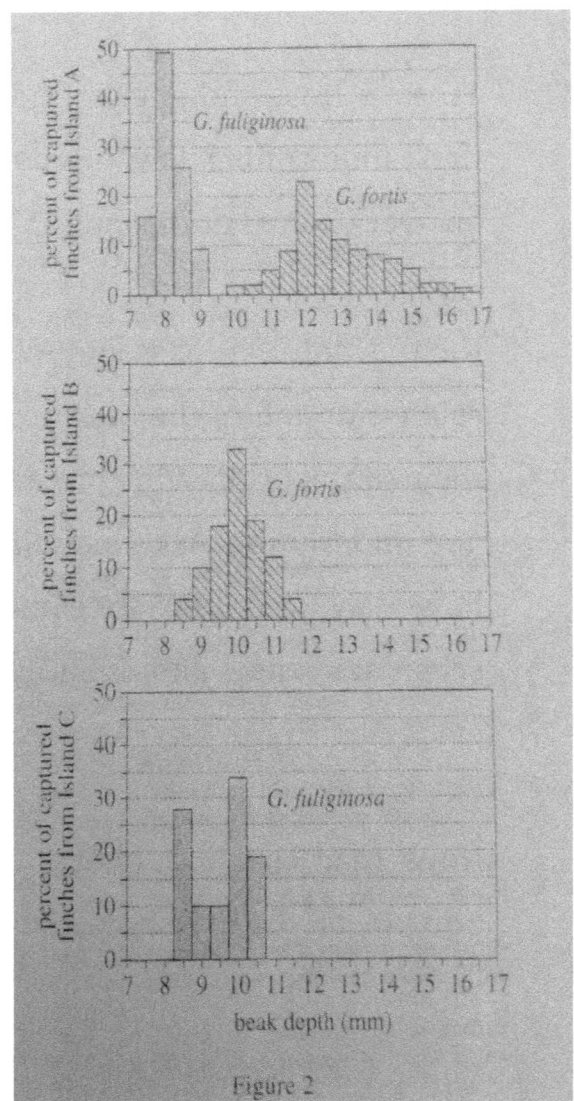

Figure 2

Study 2

After completing Study 1, the researchers returned to Island B each of the next 10 years, from 1976 to 1985. During each visit, the researchers captured at least 50 *G. fortis* finches and measured their beak depths. Then the calculated the average *G. fortis* beak depth for each of the 10 years. The researchers noted that, during the 10-year period, 3 years were exceptionally dry, and 1 year was very wet (see Figure 3). Small seeds are abundant during wet years. During dry years, all seeds are less abundant, and the average size of the available seeds is larger.

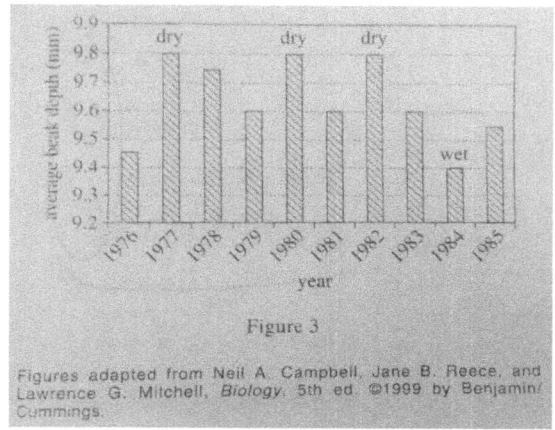

Figure 3

Figures adapted from Neil A. Campbell, Jane B. Reece, and Lawrence G. Mitchell, *Biology*, 5th ed. ©1999 by Benjamin/Cummings.

1. Based on the results of Study 1, the highest percent of finches on Island B and Island C had a beak depth of:

	Island B	Island C
A.	8 mm	8 mm
B.	9 mm	12 mm
C.	10 mm	8 mm
D.	10 mm	10 mm

2. During which of the following years were small seeds likely most abundant on Island B?
   A. 1977
   B. 1980
   C. 1982
   D. 1984

3. Study 1 differed from Study 2 in which of the following ways?

   A. *G. fortis* finches were captured during Study 1 but not during Study 2.
   B. *G. fuliginosa* finches were captured during Study 1 but not during Study 2
   C. The beak depth of captured birds was measured during Study 1 but not during Study 2.
   D. The beak depth of captured birds was measured during Study 2 but not during Study 1.

4. It is most likley that the researchers tagged the birds that they captured during Study 1 to:
   A. Determine how beak depth was affected by rainfall on Island A.
   B. Determine the average age of each finch population.
   C. Ensure that the beak depth of each finch was measured multiple times during Study 1.
   D. Ensure that the beak depth of each finch was measured only once during Study 1.

5. Based on the results of Study 2, would a finch with a beak depth of 9.4 mm or a finch with a beak depth of 9.9 mm more likely have had a greater chance of survival duirng 1977?
   A. A finch with a beak depth of 9.4 mm, because, on average, the size of available seeds is larger during dry years.
   B. A finch with a beak depth of 9.4 mm, because, on average, the size of available seeds is smaller during dry years.

C. A finch with beak depth of 9.9 mm, because, on average, the size of available seeds is larger during dry years.

D. A finch with a beak depth of 9.9 mm, because, on average, the size of available seeds is smaller during dry years.

6. A researcher hypothesized that there would be more variation in the beak depths measure for the *G. fortis* finches when they were forced to compete with another finch species for seeds. Do the results of Study 1 support this hypothesis?

A. Yes; the range of beak depths measured for *G. fortis* finches was greater on Island A than on Island B.

B. Yes; the range of beak depths measured for *G. fortis* finches was greater on Island B than on Island A.

C. No; the range of beak depths measured for *G. fortis* finches was greater on Island A than on Island B.

D. No; the range of beak depths measured for *G. fortis* finches was greater on Island B than on Island A.

Science Vocabulary

absolute zero: approximately -273 °C, the lowest-possible temperature.

acid: a compound that releases hydrogen (H+) ions when dissolved in water; has a pH less than 7.

algae: simple, one-celled plantlike organisms found in water or damp places; includes seaweeds, pond scum, and so on.

alloy: a substance composed of two or more metals.

atmosphere: the layer of air surrounding Earth.

atmospheric pressure: the pressure exerted by the atmosphere on every part of Earth's surface, approximately 10 newtons per square centimeter (10 N/cm^2).

atom: the smallest part of an element that is recognizable as that element.

barometer: an instrument that measures atmospheric pressure.

base: a compound that releases hydroxide ions (OH⁻) in water; has a pH greater than 7; is sometimes called an alkali.

boiling point: the temperature at which additional thermal energy causes a substance to change from a liquid to a vapor.

calorie: a quantity of heat energy; the amount needed to raise the temperature of one gram (1 g) of water 1 °C. The large Calorie, or "food calorie" is a kilocalorie (1000 calories).

carbohydrate: an organic compound like sugar or starch that contains carbon, hydrogen, and oxygen in the ratio of 1:2:1; the human body's main source of energy.

carcinogen: a cancer-causing agent.

carnivore: a meat eater.

catalyst: a substance that speeds up a chemical reaction without being changed by the reaction.

cell: the lowest-level structure of any living organism that can perform all of the functions of life, including reproduction.

chlorophyll: the main pigment in plants that captures light energy during photosynthesis.

compound: a substance composed of two or more chemically bonded elements.

concentration: the exact amount of substance dissolved in a given amount of solvent; refers to a solution.

condensation: the process whereby a decrease in energy cause vapor particles to return to a liquid phase.

conductor: a material that allows heat or electricity to flow through it with minimal resistance.

control: a sample in which no variables are tested, thus serving as a basis for comparison.

control variable: a variable that stays constant in an experiment, allowing the effect of another variable to be measured.

convection: the circulation of fluid caused by warm fluid

rising and cool fluid sinking.

density: in a physics sense, the amount of mass per unit volume; in a more general sense, the quantity per unit area or volume.

diffusion: the scattering of light; the spreading of a liquid or gas from areas of higher concentration to areas of lower concentration.

DNA: nucleic acid in the cells of an organism; contains the genes of the organism and transmits these to future generations.

ecological succession: a sequence of changes in the plant and/or animal life of a region over time.

electron: a negatively charged fundamental atomic particle.

element: a substance consisting of exactly one type of atom.

erosion: wearing away; typically the washing away of sand or rock by running water or wind.

evaporation: the changing of liquid into gas.

fossil: the preserved remains of a very old organism.

frequency: the number of cycles per unit time of a repeating phenomenon.

glucose: a simple sugar that is broken down to provide energy to an organism.

habitat: the part of an ecosystem where a plant or an animal naturally grows or lives.

herbivore: an animal that eats only plants.

hormone: a chemical substance secreted by a gland of the body that affects other parts of the body.

humidity: the amount of water vapor in the air.

hypothesis: a statement that is a proposed explanation of a scientific phenomenon.

infrared radiation: electromagnetic waves whose wavelength is longer than that of visible light.

insulator: a substance that blocks the flow of heat or electricity.

ion: a molecule or atom that has become charged by either gaining or losing an electron.

isotope: a variety of an element with the same number of protons per atom but a different number of neutrons.

kinetic energy: the energy of an object due to its motion.

melting point: the temperature at which additional thermal energy breaks the chemical bonds holding a substance together and causes the substance to change from the solid to the liquid state.

molecule: the smallest unit of a chemical compound.

neutron: a fundamental atomic particle that has no charge.

ore: a piece of rock from which metal can be profitably extracted.

osmosis: the movement of liquid through a membrane.

parasite: an organism that invades another organism (its host) and feeds off the host.

pH: a numerical scale from 1-14 representing the acidity or alkalinity of a solution; 1 is very acidic, 14 is very alkaline,

and 7 is neutral.

photosynthesis: the process in which plants use the sun's energy to convert carbon dioxide into water and glucose.

pressure: force per unit area.

protein: a complex molecule composed of amino acids that carries out a variety of processes in cells.

proton: a positively charged fundamental atomic particle.

starch: a complex carbohydrate found in potatoes, rice, corn, and many other vegetables.

symbiosis: a close relationship between two organisms that is mutually beneficial.

ultraviolet radiation: electromagnetic waves with wavelength shorter than that of visible light.

vapor: the gaseous form of a liquid.

X ray: electromagnetic radiation with wavelength shorter than ultraviolet radiation.

Understanding the Science Test | 58

Troubleshooting Science Tactics

For each question you missed, find the reason in the left column and write the question number in the adjacent right column.

Time? *I did not:*	Question Number	The Question? *I did not:*	Question Number	The Answer? *I did not:*	Question Number
• Spend 5 minutes on each passage		• Pay attention to the control group, variation group, or factors.		• See the answer when I skimmed the passage or reviewed the data	
• Use all of my time		• Ask what was being represented in the tables, graphs, columns, and rows.		• Recognize the answer was in a different format from the question	
• Make two passes		• Note the units of measurements.		• Guess the right answer	
• Identify the difficult or impossible questions, or spent too much time on them during the first pass		• Ask what factor varied and the result or difference between the group.		• Recognize insignificant issues in the answer choices	
• Slash the bubbles		• Look for patterns, changes, extremes, points of change, variation, or trends.		• Understand the meaning of important words	
• Stay on the grid		• Pay attention to conflicting viewpoints.			
		• Approach Conflicting Viewpoints/Principle questions like reading questions and apply Q. S. NRAF			

For each question missed, record the degree of difficulty and type of question. Write the question number in each of the categories.

Degree of Difficulty			Type of Question		
Easy	Difficult	Impossible	Experimental	Data Analysis	Principle/ Conflicting Viewpoints

Troubleshooting Science Tactics

For each question you missed, find the reason in the left column and write the question number in the adjacent right column.

Time? I did not:	Question Number	The Question? I did not:	Question Number	The Answer? I did not:	Question Number
• Spend 5 minutes on each passage		• Pay attention to the control group, variation group, or factors.		• See the answer when I skimmed the passage or reviewed the data	
• Use all of my time		• Ask what was being represented in the tables, graphs, columns, and rows.		• Recognize the answer was in a different format from the question	
• Make two passes		• Note the units of measurements.		• Guess the right answer	
• Identify the difficult or impossible questions, or spent too much time on them during the first pass		• Ask what factor varied and the result or difference between the group.		• Recognize insignificant issues in the answer choices	
• Slash the bubbles		• Look for patterns, changes, extremes, points of change, variation, or trends.		• Understand the meaning of important words	
• Stay on the grid		• Pay attention to conflicting viewpoints.			
		• Approach Conflicting Viewpoints/Principle questions like reading questions and apply Q. S. NRAF			

For each question missed, record the degree of difficulty and type of question. Write the question number in each of the categories.

Degree of Difficulty			Type of Question		
Easy	Difficult	Impossible	Experimental	Data Analysis	Principle/ Conflicting Viewpoints

Troubleshooting Science Tactics

For each question you missed, find the reason in the left column and write the question number in the adjacent right column.

Time? *I did not:*	Question Number	The Question? *I did not:*	Question Number	The Answer? *I did not:*	Question Number
• Spend 5 minutes on each passage		• Pay attention to the control group, variation group, or factors.		• See the answer when I skimmed the passage or reviewed the data	
• Use all of my time		• Ask what was being represented in the tables, graphs, columns, and rows.		• Recognize the answer was in a different format from the question	
• Make two passes		• Note the units of measurements.		• Guess the right answer	
• Identify the difficult or impossible questions, or spent too much time on them during the first pass		• Ask what factor varied and the result or difference between the group.		• Recognize insignificant issues in the answer choices	
• Slash the bubbles		• Look for patterns, changes, extremes, points of change, variation, or trends.		• Understand the meaning of important words	
• Stay on the grid		• Pay attention to conflicting viewpoints.			
		• Approach Conflicting Viewpoints/Principle questions like reading questions and apply Q. S. NRAF			

For each question missed, record the degree of difficulty and type of question. Write the question number in each of the categories.

Degree of Difficulty			Type of Question		
Easy	Difficult	Impossible	Experimental	Data Analysis	Principle/ Conflicting Viewpoints

Troubleshooting Science Tactics

For each question you missed, find the reason in the left column and write the question number in the adjacent right column.

Time? *I did not:*	Question Number	The Question? *I did not:*	Question Number	The Answer? *I did not:*	Question Number
• Spend 5 minutes on each passage		• Pay attention to the control group, variation group, or factors.		• See the answer when I skimmed the passage or reviewed the data	
• Use all of my time		• Ask what was being represented in the tables, graphs, columns, and rows.		• Recognize the answer was in a different format from the question	
• Make two passes		• Note the units of measurements.		• Guess the right answer	
• Identify the difficult or impossible questions, or spent too much time on them during the first pass		• Ask what factor varied and the result or difference between the group.		• Recognize insignificant issues in the answer choices	
• Slash the bubbles		• Look for patterns, changes, extremes, points of change, variation, or trends.		• Understand the meaning of important words	
• Stay on the grid		• Pay attention to conflicting viewpoints.			
		• Approach Conflicting Viewpoints/Principle questions like reading questions and apply Q. S. NRAF			

For each question missed, record the degree of difficulty and type of question. Write the question number in each of the categories.

Degree of Difficulty			Type of Question		
Easy	Difficult	Impossible	Experimental	Data Analysis	Principle/ Conflicting Viewpoints

Troubleshooting Science Tactics

For each question you missed, find the reason in the left column and write the question number in the adjacent right column.

Time? *I did not:*	Question Number	The Question? *I did not:*	Question Number	The Answer? *I did not:*	Question Number
• Spend 5 minutes on each passage		• Pay attention to the control group, variation group, or factors.		• See the answer when I skimmed the passage or reviewed the data	
• Use all of my time		• Ask what was being represented in the tables, graphs, columns, and rows.		• Recognize the answer was in a different format from the question	
• Make two passes		• Note the units of measurements.		• Guess the right answer	
• Identify the difficult or impossible questions, or spent too much time on them during the first pass		• Ask what factor varied and the result or difference between the group.		• Recognize insignificant issues in the answer choices	
• Slash the bubbles		• Look for patterns, changes, extremes, points of change, variation, or trends.		• Understand the meaning of important words	
• Stay on the grid		• Pay attention to conflicting viewpoints.			
		• Approach Conflicting Viewpoints/Principle questions like reading questions and apply Q. S. NRAF			

For each question missed, record the degree of difficulty and type of question. Write the question number in each of the categories.

Degree of Difficulty			Type of Question		
Easy	Difficult	Impossible	Experimental	Data Analysis	Principle/ Conflicting Viewpoints

Quick Facts

- Timing: You will have 45 minutes for 75 questions. This is an average of 30 seconds per question. There are five passages, so you will have 9 minutes to complete each passage and set of questions. Think of it as 5, nine-minute tests. Do not borrow time from one passage to another.
- Knowledge tested: punctuation grammar, sentence structure, organization, and style.
- English is easier, so you must get more questions right to achieve your goal score for the English test.
- A portion of the passage will be underlined and you will have four choices addressing what to do with that portion.
- These are the directions. Read them now so that you do not need to take time to read them during the test:

> Directions: *In the five passages that follow, certain words and phrases are underlined and numbered. In the right-hand column, you will find alternatives for the underlined part. In most cases, you are to choose the one that best expresses the idea, makes the statement appropriate for the standard written English, or is worded most consistently with the style and tone of the passage as a whole. If you think the original version is best, choose "NO CHANGE." In some cases, you will find in the right-hand column a question about the underlined part. You are to choose the best answer to the question. You*

will also find questions about a section of the passage, or about the passage as a whole. These questions do not refer to an underlined portion of the passage, but rather are identified by a number or numbers in a box. For each question, choose the alternative you consider best and fill in the corresponding oval on your answer document. Read each passage through once before you begin to answer the questions that accompany it. For many of the questions, you must read several sentences beyond the question to determine the answer. Be sure that you have read far enough ahead each time you choose an alternative.

Types of Questions

1. Less is More… Points

Approximately 20 questions, or one-third of the English test, relate to concise writing. Concise writing deals with redundancy, verbosity, and relevance.

In Less is More… Points, "OMIT" or "DELETE" is usually an answer choice.

Redundancy is repeating something that has already been stated. Two statements in the passage will be worded differently, but will have the same meaning.

Verbosity is the use of too many words. Verbose sentences are often awkward. If you find yourself rereading a sentence because you did not understand its meaning, this may be a clue that the sentence is verbose.

Relevance asks whether the underlined portion is connected or pertinent to the rest of the passage.

Example of redundancy

| China was certainly one of the cradles of civilization. <u>It's obvious that, China has a long history.</u> As is the case with other ancient cultures, the early history of China is lost in mythology. | F. NO CHANGE
G. It's obvious that China has a long history.
H. Obviously; China has a long history.
J. OMIT the underlined portion. |

"OMIT the underlined portion" is an answer choice, and alerts you this may be a Less is More... Points question. The underlined portion, <u>It's obvious that, China has a long history.</u> restates the first sentence, "China was certainly one of the cradles of civilization." The underlined portion is redundant.

Example of verbosity

Brightly lit stations welcomed the public, many of whom <u>that were</u> skeptical of traveling underground.	F. NO CHANGE G. were fearful and H. though they J. OMIT the underlined portion.

Again, "OMIT the underlined portion" is an answer choice, and alerts you this is a Less is More... Points question. The varying length of the answer choices is another clue. The word "that" adds nothing to the sentence and may cause you to stumble in your comprehension. The sentence is verbose and the underlined portion should be omitted.

Example of relevance

The original subway line was 9.1 miles long and had twenty-eight stations. The first train ran from City Hall to West 145th Street <u>in under a half an hour</u>. Tens of thousands of New Yorkers could now avoid traffic jams.	A. NO CHANGE B. in the completion of its route. C. in twenty-six minutes. D. DELETE the underlined portion and end the sentence with a period.

Again, deleting the underlined portion is an answer choice. We know from the first sentence that the topic of the passage is the original subway line. The time of the running of the first train is related, but not pertinent to the topic. Choice D – delete the underlined portion – is the correct answer.

2. Reason/Logic Questions

The second type of question is reason and logic questions. There are approximately 20 questions – again, about one-third of the English Test – that ask about logic and sense.

3. Grammar (Usage/Mechanics)

Questions in this category test your understanding of punctuation, agreement between subject and verb, agreement between pronoun and antecedent, agreement between modifiers and the modified word, verb formation, pronoun case, formation of comparative and superlative adjectives and adverbs, and idiomatic usage.

4. Nonstandard English

These questions relate to judging the passage as a whole. In these questions, you will be tested for meaning, purpose, tone, overall organization, and style.

Tactics for Understanding the English Test

1. Spend 6-7 minutes on the first pass through each passage. Spend 2-3 minutes on the second pass.

2. Despite the directions, do not read the entire passage before answering. Rather, read the passage through the first or next underlined portion.

3. Read the question and the answer choices.

4. Ask yourself: Is this a Less is More... Points question? That is, is it redundant, verbose, or irrelevant? Two clues alert you to Less is More... Points questions:
    a. The length of the answer choices vary greatly,
    b. "Omit" or "delete" are answer choices.

If you judge it as a Less is More... Points question, the shortest answer is usually the best. **When in doubt, take it out.**

5. If it is not a Less is More... Points question, ask yourself: Is this a Reason/Logic question? Does it make sense? If it does not make sense, select the answer that turns the underlined portion into sense, and move on.

6. If it is not a Reason/Logic question, ask yourself: Is this a Grammar question? Does it sound like English? If it is a Grammar

question, select the answer that corrects the error, and move on.

7. If it is none of the above and the question relates to the passage as a whole, it is a Nonstandard English question. Because it requires reading the entire passage, it should be answered on the second pass.

Application of English Tactics

Work through the following sample English passage, applying the tactics as you go. Take as much time as you need, and refer back often to the previous tactics.

Dragonfly

The nature trail is six feet wide and seven miles long. It slithers through the forest like a snake curving, and bending along the banks [1] of the river.

The county cleared this path and paved it with pack gravel, so they [2] [3] would have a peaceful place to hike and bike.

I ride this trail nearly every day – not on a bike, but on "Luigi". [4] That's the nickname I gave my motorized wheelchair. [5]

1. A. NO CHANGE
   B. snake, curving and bending
   C. snake curving and bending,
   D. snake, curving, and bending,

2. Which of the following alternatives to the underlined portion would NOT be acceptable?
   F. path, paving
   G. path and then paved
   H. path before paving
   J. path paved

3. A. NO CHANGE
   B. knowing they
   C. that they
   D. people

4. F. NO CHANGE
   G. day; not on a bike
   H. day not on a bike
   J. day, not on a bike;

5. If the writer were to delete the preceding sentence, the essay would primarily lose:
   A. a reason why the narrator is in the forest.
   B. a detail important for understanding the essay.
   C. a contrast to the lighthearted tone of the essay.
   D. nothing at all; this information is irrelevant to the essay.

Today, Luigi's battery is fully charged, [6]

I know I can go all the way to the end of the trail and back. But I always carry a cell phone on me just in case. Luigi's motor moves slowly [7] as we venture along the trail. I can hear the gravel quietly crunching beneath Luigi's rubber wheels. I hear [8] the songs of cardinals in the trees and the clamor of crickets in the grasses. I hear the murmur of water slipping over time-smoothed rocks. It is [9] September, and some of the trees are starting to blush red and orange at their tips. The wind ruffles my hair and chills my face as I bounce gently, along [10] in my padded chair.

6. F. NO CHANGE
G. charged, because of that,
H. charged, this means that
J. charged, so

7. Which choice would most logically and effectively emphasize the positive, friendly attitude the narrator has toward Luigi?
A. NO CHANGE
B. travels safely
C. proceeds carefully
D. purrs softly

8. F. NO CHANGE
G. You can hear
H. One can even hear
J. While hearing

9. A. NO CHANGE
B. Due to the fact that it is
C. It turns into the month of
D. Because it has turned into

10. F. NO CHANGE
G. gentle, along
H. gently along
J. gentle along,

Bicyclists streak past in a blur [11] of color and a cloud of dust [12] I don't understand their hurry. Luigi can go fast, but I like to ride slowly, to see like a hovering dragonfly. I want to see everything that has changed, grown, bloomed, or died since yesterday. Today I notice that a spider has woven a web between some honeysuckle bushes by the bridge. I see that the bank of vibrant yellow black-eyed Susans by the barbed wire fence is starting to dry and fade away. I spend an hour; looking and listening and learning. [13]

11. Which choice most effectively leads into the new subject of the paragraph?
A. NO CHANGE
B. The sun begins to set
C. Nature always impresses me
D. Days can go by quickly

12. F. NO CHANGE
G. dust, however,
H. dust.
J. dust,

13. A. NO CHANGE
B. hour, looking,
C. hour looking;
D. hour looking

Troubleshooting English Tactics

For each question you missed, find the reason in the left column and write the question number in the adjacent right column.

Time? *I did not:*	Question Number	The Type of Question?	Question Number	The Answer? *I did not:*	Question Number
• Spend 9 minutes on each passage		• Less is More… Points - Redundant, verbose, relevance		• See the answer when I skimmed the passage	
• Use all of my time		• Reason/Logic		• Recognize the answer was in a different format from the question	
• Make two passes		• Nonstandard English		• Guess the right answer	
• Identify the difficult or impossible questions, or spent too much time on them during the first pass		• Punctuation		• Recognize insignificant issues in the answer choices	
• Slash the bubbles		• Capitalization		• Understand the meaning of important words	
• Stay on the grid		• Usage (using the right word)			
		• Parts of speech			
		• Sentence construction			
		• Agreement			
		• Other Grammar			

Troubleshooting English Tactics

For each question you missed, find the reason in the left column and write the question number in the adjacent right column.

Time? *I did not:*	Question Number	The Type of Question?	Question Number	The Answer? *I did not:*	Question Number
• Spend 9 minutes on each passage		• Less is More... Points - Redundant, verbose, relevance		• See the answer when I skimmed the passage	
• Use all of my time		• Reason/Logic		• Recognize the answer was in a different format from the question	
• Make two passes		• Nonstandard English		• Guess the right answer	
• Identify the difficult or impossible questions, or spent too much time on them during the first pass		• Punctuation		• Recognize insignificant issues in the answer choices	
• Slash the bubbles		• Capitalization		• Understand the meaning of important words	
• Stay on the grid		• Usage (using the right word)			
		• Parts of speech			
		• Sentence construction			
		• Agreement			
		• Other Grammar			

Troubleshooting English Tactics

For each question you missed, find the reason in the left column and write the question number in the adjacent right column.

Time? *I did not:*	Question Number	The Type of Question?	Question Number	The Answer? *I did not:*	Question Number
• Spend 9 minutes on each passage		• Less is More... Points - Redundant, verbose, relevance		• See the answer when I skimmed the passage	
• Use all of my time		• Reason/Logic		• Recognize the answer was in a different format from the question	
• Make two passes		• Nonstandard English		• Guess the right answer	
• Identify the difficult or impossible questions, or spent too much time on them during the first pass		• Punctuation		• Recognize insignificant issues in the answer choices	
• Slash the bubbles		• Capitalization		• Understand the meaning of important words	
• Stay on the grid		• Usage (using the right word)			
		• Parts of speech			
		• Sentence construction			
		• Agreement			
		• Other Grammar			

Troubleshooting English Tactics

For each question you missed, find the reason in the left column and write the question number in the adjacent right column.

Time? *I did not:*	Question Number	The Type of Question?	Question Number	The Answer? *I did not:*	Question Number
• Spend 9 minutes on each passage		• Less is More... Points - Redundant, verbose, relevance		• See the answer when I skimmed the passage	
• Use all of my time		• Reason/Logic		• Recognize the answer was in a different format from the question	
• Make two passes		• Nonstandard English		• Guess the right answer	
• Identify the difficult or impossible questions, or spent too much time on them during the first pass		• Punctuation		• Recognize insignificant issues in the answer choices	
• Slash the bubbles		• Capitalization		• Understand the meaning of important words	
• Stay on the grid		• Usage (using the right word)			
		• Parts of speech			
		• Sentence construction			
		• Agreement			
		• Other Grammar			

Troubleshooting English Tactics

For each question you missed, find the reason in the left column and write the question number in the adjacent right column.

Time? *I did not:*	Question Number	The Type of Question?	Question Number	The Answer? *I did not:*	Question Number
• Spend 9 minutes on each passage		• Less is More… Points - Redundant, verbose, relevance		• See the answer when I skimmed the passage	
• Use all of my time		• Reason/Logic		• Recognize the answer was in a different format from the question	
• Make two passes		• Nonstandard English		• Guess the right answer	
• Identify the difficult or impossible questions, or spent too much time on them during the first pass		• Punctuation		• Recognize insignificant issues in the answer choices	
• Slash the bubbles		• Capitalization		• Understand the meaning of important words	
• Stay on the grid		• Usage (using the right word)			
		• Parts of speech			
		• Sentence construction			
		• Agreement			
		• Other Grammar			

Quick Facts

• You will have 60 minutes to answer 60 questions; an average of one minute per question.

• The questions get progressively more difficult (but this is subjective to your strengths).

• Questions are easy, difficult, and impossible. You get to be the judge of the difficulty of each question.

• Easy questions, of which there are many, have few words and are direct (x + x + x =).

• Difficult questions test your understanding of logical reasoning ability.

• There are five answer choices. The choice "cannot be determined" is almost NEVER the correct answer.

• Read the directions now so that you do not need to take time to read them again during the test.

> Directions: *"Solve each problem, choose the correct answer, and then fill in the corresponding oval on your answer document. Do not linger over problems that take too much time. Solve as many as you can; then return to the others in the time you have left for this test. You are permitted to use a calculator on this test. You may use your calculator for any problems you choose, but some of the problems may best be done without using a calculator. Note: Unless otherwise stated, all of the following should be assumed:*
>   a. *Illustrative figures are NOT necessarily drawn to scale.*

b. *Geometric figures lie in a plane.*

c. *The word line indicates a straight line.*

d. *The word average indicates arithmetic mean.*

Math Subjects Covered

Pre-algebra (14 questions)

This includes numbers, fractions, decimals, positive powers, square roots, ratios and proportions, percent, multiples, factors, absolute value, order, simple equations, probability, counting, and simple statistics.

Elementary Algebra (9 questions)

These questions contain variables, substitution, simple operations on polynomials, factoring, quadratic equations solved by factoring, linear equations, inequalities, exponents, and square roots.

Intermediate Algebra (9 questions)

Intermediate Algebra questions test your knowledge of quadratic formulas, rational expressions, radicals, inequalities, absolute value, sequences, simultaneous equations, quadratic inequalities, functions, matrices, roots of polynomials, complex numbers, and functions.

Coordinate Geometry (9 questions)

These questions include number line, xy- plane, graphs of polynomials, circles, curves in the xy-plane, equations, slopes, parallel and perpendicular lines, distances, midpoints, transformations, and conic sections.

Plane Geometry (14 questions)

This includes triangles, rectangles, parallelograms, circles, angles, parallel and perpendicular lines, transformations, techniques of proof, simple three-dimensional geometry, perimeter, area, and volume.

Trigonometry (4 questions)

This Math section includes 4 questions that test your knowledge of trigonometry, including right triangle trigonometry, radians, graphs, identities, equations, sine and cosine.

If your goal is to get the most number of questions right, then your time should be spent mastering pre-algebra and plane geometry concepts and questions, as these make up 47% of the Math questions. Conversely, unless you are a trig-wiz, do not use your time trying to prepare for the four trigonometry questions.

Types of Questions

Diagram questions

These are questions related to drawings and visual aids.

Story questions

Story questions will require you to read a short passage and extract the math problem from it.

Concept questions

Concept questions will test your logical reasoning ability. These are usually difficult questions, so they are typically answered on the second pass.

Tactics for Understanding the Math Test

1. Two-Pass Method

As with the other subject tests, you will make two passes through the Math test. Because of the number of questions, this method is most critical for the Math test.

Allow 45 minutes for the first pass, including filling in the slashed bubbles. With each question, ask yourself: Is this problem easy, difficult, or impossible? Impossible questions are those that will take significantly longer than one minute to solve. During the first pass:

- o Answer the easy questions.
- o Guess on the impossible questions.
- o Mark the difficult questions and come back to them on the second pass.

Allow 15 minutes for the second pass, including filling in the slashed bubbles.

- Pick up the difficult questions skipped on first pass.
- If you are running out of time, look for questions you can answer.
- In the last few minutes, guess on unanswered questions. Select a letter such as *C/H* and stick with it for all of the remaining unanswered questions.

2. Grasp, Evaluate, Elect (GEE)

The second tactic is to grasp, evaluate and elect.

Step 1: Grasp. Focus on the question and what is being asked for; rephrase it if necessary. Ask yourself: What kind of problem is this? What am I looking for? What am I given?

Step 2: Evaluate. What is the quickest way to solve this problem?

Step 3: Elect. When you cannot answer or if you are stuck, check the answer choices, and select the one that you think works.

Example

If the sum of five consecutive even integers is equal to their product, what is the greatest of the five integers?

      A. 4
      B. 8

C. 14

D. 16

E. 24

Step 1: Grasp

Before you can begin to solve this problem, you have to figure out what it is asking, and to do that, you need to know the meaning of sum, product, consecutive, even, and integer. Put the question into words that you can understand. What the question is really saying here is that when you add up these five consecutive even integers, you get the same answer as when you multiply them.

Step 2: Evaluate

How are you going to determine these five integers? Set up an equation:

$$x + (x - 2) + (x - 4) + (x - 6) + (x - 8) = x(x - 2)(x - 4)(x - 6)(x - 8)$$

But there is no way that you will have time to solve an equation like this. So do not even try. Come up with a better way.

Stop and think logically for a moment. When you think about sums and products, it is natural to think mostly of positive integers. With positive integers, you would generally expect the product to be greater than the sum.

But what about negative integers? The sum of five negatives is negative, and the product of five negatives is also negative. Generally, the product will be "more negative" than the sum, so with negative integers the product will be less than the sum.

The product and sum will be the same at the boundary of positive and negative; around 0. The five consecutive even integers with equal product and sum are: -4, -2, 0, 2, and 4.

(-4) x (-2) x 0 x 2 x 4 = (-4) + (-2) + 0 + 2 + 4

The product and sum are both 0.

Step 3: Elect
The question asks for the greatest of the five integers, which is 4, choice F.

3. Creative Solutions
When you get stuck or run out of time, find the quickest way to solve the problem. Here are some techniques that you can use to find creative solutions:
- **Back solve** and try out each answer choice until you find one that works.
- Pick numbers to temporarily **replace** variables.

- **Guesstimate** if you understand what the problem is asking for, but don't know which formula to apply, figure out a ballpark estimate, and select the answer that is closest.
- **Eyeball** diagrams. Despite directions, diagrams are often drawn to scale. Size it up with your eyes.

Example of Guesstimate

When you understand a problem but cannot figure out how to solve it, you can at least get a general idea of how big the answer is. This is sometimes called a "guesstimate".

Here is a question that is not hard to understand but is hard to solve if you do not remember the rules for simplifying and adding radicals.

$$\frac{\sqrt{32} + \sqrt{24}}{\sqrt{8}} = ?$$

A. $\sqrt{7}$
B. $\sqrt{2} + \sqrt{3}$
C. $2 + \sqrt{3}$
D. $\sqrt{2} + 3$
E. 7

Step 1: Grasp

The question wants you to simplify the given expression, which includes three radicals. Turn the radicals into numbers that you can use, then work out the fraction.

Step 2: Evaluate

The best way to solve this problem would be to apply the rules of radicals – but if you do not remember them, you can still guesstimate. In the question, the numbers under the radicals are not too far away from perfect squares. You could round $\sqrt{32}$ off to $\sqrt{36}$, which is 6. You could round $\sqrt{24}$ off to $\sqrt{25}$, which is 5. And you could round $\sqrt{8}$ off to $\sqrt{9}$, which is 3. So the expression is now $\frac{6+5}{3}$, which is $3\frac{2}{3}$. That is just a guesstimate; the actual value might be something a bit less or a bit more than that.

Step 3: Elect

Now look at the answer choices. Choice A is less than 3, so it is too small. Choice B is about 1.4 + 1.7, or just barely more than 3, so it seems a little small, too. Choice C is about 2 + 1.7, or about 3.7 – that is very close to our guesstimate! We still have to check the other choices, though. Choice D is about 1.4 + 3, or 4.4 – too big. And choice E, 7, is obviously way too big. Looks like our best bet is C – and C in fact is the correct answer.

Example of Eyeballing

There is another simple but powerful tactic that should give you

at least a 50/50 chance on almost any diagram question: Trust common sense and careful thinking. For almost half of all diagram questions, you can get a reasonable answer without solving for anything. Just eyeball it.

The math directions say, "Illustrative figures are NOT necessarily drawn to scale," but in fact, they almost always are. You are never really supposed to just eyeball the figure, but it makes a lot more sense than random guessing. Occasionally, eyeballing can help you narrow down the choices.

In the figure below, points A, B, and C lie on a circle centered at O. Triangle AOC is equilateral, and the length of OC is 3 inches. What is the length, in inches, of arc ABC?

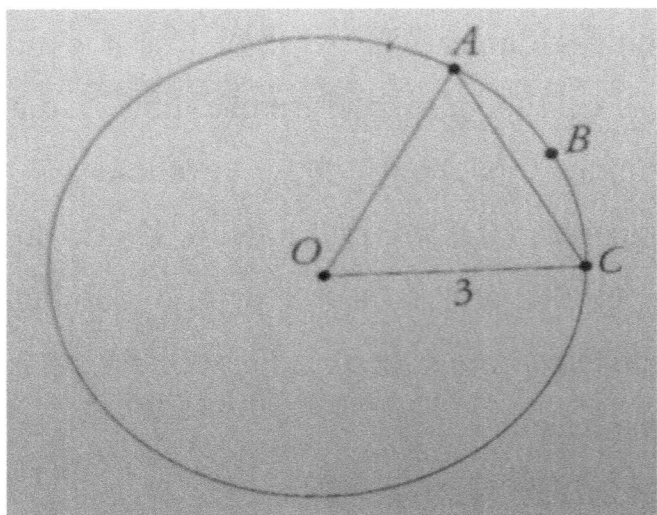

F. 3

G. π

H. 2π

J. 3π

K. 6π

Step 1: Grasp

There is an "equilateral" triangle that connects the center and two points on the circumference of a circle. You are looking for the length of the arc that goes from A to C.

Step 2: Evaluate

What you are "supposed" to do to answer this question is recall and apply the formula for the length of an arc. But suppose you do not remember that formula.

You can eyeball it. If you understand the question well enough to realize that "equilateral" means all sides are equal, then you know immediately that side $\overline{AC}$ is 3 inches long. Now look at arc ABC compared to side $\overline{AC}$. Suppose you were an insect and you had to walk from A to C. If you walked along line segment $\overline{AC}$, it would be a 3-inch trip. About how long of a walk would it be along arc ABC? Clearly more, but not much more, than 3 inches.

Step 3: Elect

Now look at the answer choices. Choice F is no good: You know the arc is more than 3 inches. All the other choices are in terms of π. Just think of π as "a bit more than 3" and you will quickly see that only one answer choice is in the right ballpark. Choice G – π –

would be "a bit more than 3," which sounds pretty good. Choice H - 2π – would be "something more than 6." Already that is way too big. Choices J and K are even bigger. The answer has to be G.

Tactics for Question Types

Diagram Questions

Use the drawing to help find the answer.

Story Questions

Put the information in real numbers or simpler situations.

Concept Questions

Zoom out and see the big picture and think abstractly. Know math vocabulary. Be familiar with the following math lingo:

- *"Integers" include 0 and negative whole numbers.* If a questions says "x and y are integers," it is not ruling out numbers like 0 and -1.
- *"Evens and odds" include 0 and negative whole numbers.* Zero and -2 are even numbers, -1 is an odd number.
- *"Prime numbers" do not include 1.* The technical definition of a prime number is: "A positive integer with exactly two distinct positive integer factors." Two is prime because it has exactly two positive factors: 1 and 2. Four is not prime because it has three positive factors (1, 2, and 4). And 1 is not prime because it only has one positive factor (1), which is too few.

- *"Remainders" are integers.* If a question asks for the remainder when 15 is divided by 2, do not say "15 divided by 2 is 7.5, so the remainder is .5." What you should say is: "15 divided by 2 is 7 with a remainder of 1."
- *The $\sqrt{}$ symbol represents the positive square root only.* The equation $x^2 = 9$ has two solutions: 3 and -3. But when you see $\sqrt{9}$, it means positive 3 only.
- *"Rectangles" include squares.* The definition of a rectangle is a four-sided figure with four right angles. It does not matter if the length and width are the same. If it has four right angles, it is a rectangle. When a question refers to "rectangle ABCD," it is not ruling out a square.

Calculators and formulas:

- Know basic formulas, skills, and relationships.
- If a formula is required, the ACT test will provide it.
- If you find yourself doing extensive calculations or complex formulas, you are probably going down the wrong path.
- Check the ACT website before the test to know which calculators are allowed. What is allowed can change from time to time.

1. Tanya used $4\frac{5}{8}$ yards of fabric to make her dress and she used $1\frac{1}{3}$ yards of fabric to make her jacket. What was the total amount, in yards, that Tanya used for the complete outfit of dress and jacket?

   A. $5\frac{1}{8}$
   B. $5\frac{1}{4}$
   C. $5\frac{6}{11}$
   D. $5\frac{1}{2}$
   E. $5\frac{23}{24}$

2. $4x^3y^6 \cdot 6y^2 \cdot 2xy$ is equivalent to

   F. $12x^3y^8$
   G. $12x^4y^7$
   H. $48x^3y^6$
   I. $48x^3y^8$
   J. $48x^4y^9$

3. Brandy earns $9.50 an hour in a summer job. She is saving to buy a television set that cost $495.00. What is the least number of hours she must work, to the nearest hour, in order to save up enough to buy the television set?

   A. 52
   B. 53
   C. 55
   D. 57
   E. 60

4. If $5 + \sqrt{x - 5} = 10$, then $x =$?

   F. 4
   G. 5
   H. 10
   I. 30
   J. 50

5. A container of a substance contains 460 grams of the substance. If one unit is $1\frac{3}{5}$ cups and 1 cup of the substance weighs 8.32 grams, what is the maximum number of complete units contained in the container?

   A. 736
   B. 56
   C. 55
   D. 35
   E. 34

6. A scale drawing of a parking lot has $\frac{1}{4}$ inch representing 60 feet. If one side of the parking lot is 80 feet, what is the side length, in inches, on the scale drawing?

F. $\frac{1}{3}$
G. $\frac{3}{4}$
H. 1
I. $1\frac{1}{4}$
J. 3

7. $4x \cdot (6x)^3 = ?$

A. $864x^4$
B. $216x^3$
C. $216x^4$
D. $24x^4$
E. $18x^3$

8. Solve for n: $9n - 6 = 4n + 26$

F. 32
G. $\frac{32}{5}$
H. $\frac{32}{13}$
I. $\frac{13}{20}$
J. $\frac{13}{5}{32}$

9. A jar contains 3 red beans and 5 white beans. Two beans are randomly removed. What is the probability that these two are both white?

A. $3\dfrac{1}{42}$

B. $\dfrac{20}{56}$

C. $\dfrac{16}{49}$

D. $\dfrac{5}{8}$

E. $\dfrac{1}{2}$

10. What is the real number value of $m^2 + \sqrt{3m}$ when $5m^2 = 45$?

F. 9
G. 12
H. 25
I. 28.87
J. 33.66

11. In the figure below, the circle with center P is inscribed in $\triangle ABC$. The length of AB is 5, the length of BD is 2, and the length of DC is 4. What is the length of ED?

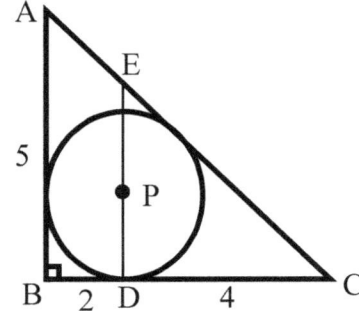

A. 3

B. $3\frac{1}{3}$
C. 4π
D. $\sqrt{61}$
E. $5\frac{1}{6}$

12. There are 10 green, 7 red, and 8 blue in a box. If one is chosen at random from the box, what is the probability that it is NOT green?

F. $\frac{2}{5}$
G. $\frac{3}{5}$
H. $\frac{2}{3}$
I. 10
J. 15

13. $\begin{bmatrix} 2 & 6 & 3 \\ 5 & 0 & 4 \end{bmatrix} \begin{bmatrix} 2 & 1 \\ -3 & 4 \\ 1 & -2 \end{bmatrix} = ?$

A. Undefined for the given matrix

B. $\begin{bmatrix} 14 & -3 \\ -11 & 26 \end{bmatrix}$

C. $\begin{bmatrix} -11 & 20 \\ 14 & -3 \end{bmatrix}$

D. $\begin{bmatrix} 2 & 12 & 3 \\ 5 & 0 & -8 \end{bmatrix}$

E. $\begin{bmatrix} 5 & 0 & -8 \\ 2 & 12 & 3 \end{bmatrix}$

Use the following table to answer questions 14-15:

The table below shows the genres of radio music, broken down by the medium, (AM, FM, or satellite) on which it is aired. In addition, the table shows the number of hours in which there is a "live" disc jockey.

Genre	Medium	# of hours where there is a "Live" Disc Jockey
Classical	AM	6
Classical	FM	3
Classical	Satellite	12
Counry	AM	24
Counry	FM	7
Counry	Satellite	16
News	AM	24
News	FM	24
News	Satellite	24
Pop	FM	14
Pop	Satellite	5
Rock	FM	12
Rock	Satellite	24

14. What is the average number of hours, rounded to the nearest hour, that the Classical genre has a "Live" disc jockey?

F. 3
G. 7
H. 14
I. 16
J. 24

15. The time of day in which there is a "live" disc jockey does not matter; as long as there is a "live" disc jockey for the number of hours listed in the table. Assume that a disc jockey can switch from any genre and medium to another with the flip of a switch. Based on the table above, what is the minimum number of disc jockeys needed, if each works a 9-hour shift?

A. 5
B. 13
C. 21
D. 22
E. 195

16. In the table below, every row, column, and diagonal must have equivalent sums. What is the value of the lower left cell in order for this to be true?

$2m$	$-8m$	$6m$
$4m$	0	$-4m$
	$8m$	$-2m$

F. $-8m$
G. $-6m$
H. -6
I. 0
J. $2m$

17. The standard coordinate plane is shown below, with the four quadrants labeled. Point R, denoted by $R(x,y)$ is graphed on this plane, such that $x \neq 0$ and $y \neq 0$.

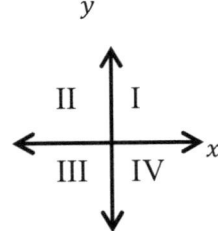

If the product xy is a negative number, then point R is located in:

A. Quadrant I only
B. Quadrant II only
C. Quadrant III only
D. Quadrant II or IV only
E. Quadrant I or III only

18. Mark spent $\frac{1}{5}$ of the project budget on binders, $\frac{1}{4}$ of what was left on pens, $\frac{1}{3}$ of what was left (after the binders and the pens purchase) on paper, and $\frac{1}{2}$ of what was finally left on name tags. He then had $12.00 left over. What was the project budget?

F. $120
G. $100
H. $80
I. $60
J. $20

19. Casey watched a movie on television from 2 P.M. until 4:15 P.M. From 2 P.M. until 2:45 P.M., there were 15 minutes of commercials. From 2:45 P.M. until 3:30 P.M. there were 25 minutes of commercials. From 3:30 P.M. until 4:15 P.M. there were 5 minutes of commercials. What percent of the movie viewing time was taken up by commercials?
   A. 20%
   B. 25%
   C. 33%
   D. 45%
   E. 50%

20. What is the length, in inches, of the diagonal of a rectangle whose dimensions are 12 inches by 16 inches?
   F. 25
   G. 14
   H. 20
   I. 200
   J. 400

21. For all x for which the expression is defined, $\dfrac{3x^2 - 3x - 18}{3x^2 - 27}$ simplifies to:
   A. $1\dfrac{2}{3}$
   B. 1
   C. $\dfrac{x-2}{x-3}$
   D. $\dfrac{x+2}{x+3}$
   E. $\dfrac{2(x+2)}{x+3}$

22. Which of the following equations is equivalent to $3x + 2y = 18$?

F. $y = -\frac{3}{2}x + 18$

G. $y = -\frac{2}{3}x + 9$

H. $y = \frac{3}{2}x + 9$

I. $y = -\frac{3}{2}x + 9$

J. $y = -\frac{2}{3}x + 9$

23. Which of the following represents an equation for which the sum of its roots is -5 and the product of its roots is 4?

A. $x^2 + 5x - 4 = 0$
B. $x^2 + 5x + 4 = 0$
C. $x^2 - 5x + 2 = 0$
D. $2x^2 + 10x - 2 = 0$
E. $x^2 - 5x + 4 = 0$

24. Given right triangle $\triangle QRS$ below, what is the value of sin Q?

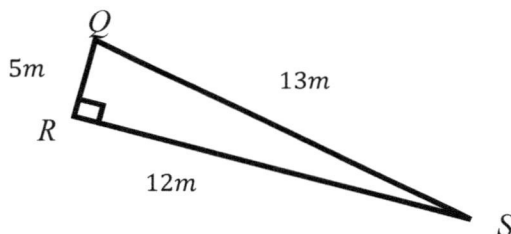

F. $\frac{5}{13}$

G. $\frac{5}{12}$

H. $\frac{12}{13}$

I. $\frac{13}{12}$

J. $\frac{12}{5}$

25. QRST is a parallelogram, and the angles are as marked:

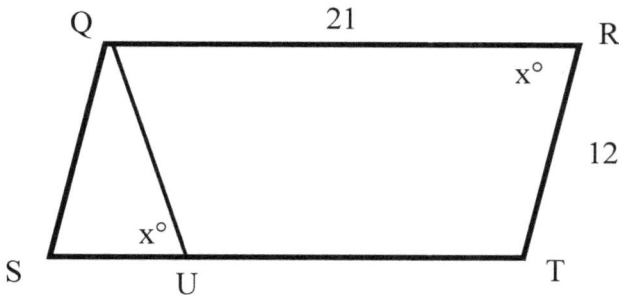

What is the value of QU?

A. 12
B. 21
C. 24.2
D. 17.2
E. 10

26. A cellphone company charges $2 per GB for the first 5 GB, $4 per GB for the next 10 GB, and $5 per GB for any GBs over 15 GB. What will the company charge for 40 GB?

F. $80
G. $160
H. $175
I. $200
J. $425

27. What is the minimum value of the expression $3 \cos 3\theta$?

A. -4
B. -3
C. -1
D. 3
E. 4

28. In right triangle $\triangle DEF$ below, the measure of segment DE is 38 inches, and the tangent of angle D is $\frac{7}{8}$. What is the length of segment EF, to the nearest hundredth of an inch?

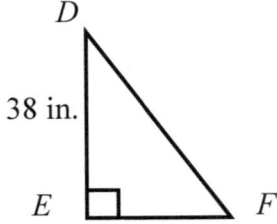

F. 33.25
G. 38.875
H. 43.40
I. 60.80
J. 190.00

29. What is the average of the expressions $5x - 12$, $3x - 7$, and $-2x + 17$?

A. $x + \frac{2}{3}$
B. $x + 1$
C. $2x - \frac{2}{3}$
D. $2x + 3$
E. $3x + 3\frac{1}{3}$

30. Consider points A, B, C, and D as shown below. AB, BC and CD are all positive integer lengths, and the length of AD is 24. If the ratio of AB to BC is 2:1, which of the following is NOT a possible length of CD?

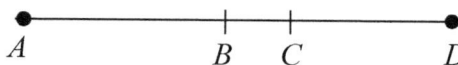

F. 9
G. 15
H. 18
I. 21
J. 24

31. If $2x + 2y = 16$, $x + 2z = 25$, and $y + z = 13$, then what is the arithmetic mean of x, y and z?

A. 6
B. $\dfrac{16}{3}$
C. 18
D. 14
E. 5

32. In the complex numbers where $i^2 = -1$, $\dfrac{i+2}{i} = $?

F. -2
G. -2-i
H. 1-2i
I. 1+2i
J. -1+2i

33. What is the area, in square millimeters, of the parallelogram *RSTU* shown below?

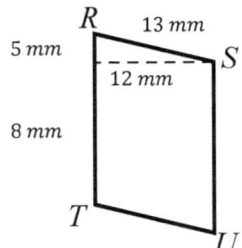

A. 30
B. 38
C. 52
D. 156
E. 169

34. For which of the following functions is $f(x) = f(-x)$?

F. $f(x) = x - 12$
G. $f(x) = x^3$
H. $f(x) = -x$
I. $f(x) = x^6 - x + 2$
J. $f(x) = -x^4 + 7$

35. Shown below is a partial map of Newtown, showing 60 square miles – a total of 6 miles of Main Street and a total of 10 miles of Big Street. There is a grocery story at the corner of Main and Big St, shown as point G. The town wants to build a new grocery store exactly halfway between the convention center, at C, and the school, at S. What would be the driving directions to get from the current grocery store to the new grocery store, by way of Main and Coal streets?

*Note: All streets and avenues shown intersect at right angles.

A. 6 miles east, 10 miles north
B. 2 miles west, 4 miles north
C. 2 miles east, 6 miles south
D. 4 miles west, 4 miles south
E. 4 miles west, 6 miles south

36. If $x - 4y$ is 60% of $5y$, what is the value of $\dfrac{x}{y}$?

F. 60
G. 18
H. 7
I. $\dfrac{18}{5}$
J. $\dfrac{3}{5}$

37. A ladder leans against a wall. If the ladder is 15 meters and the distance from the foot of the ladder to the wall is 9 meters, how high, in meters, up the wall does the ladder reach?

   A. 3
   B. 6
   C. 9
   D. 12
   E. 15

38. In the figure below, the sides of the square are tangent to the inner circle, if the area of the circle is 25π square units, what is the unit length of a side of the square?

   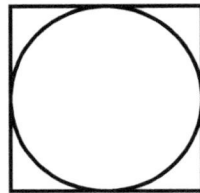

   F. 100
   G. 25
   H. 10
   I. 5
   J. π

39. The rectangles *ABCD* and *EFGH* shown below are similar. Using the given information, what is the length of side *EH*, to the nearest tenth of an inch?

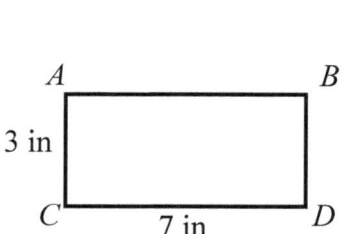
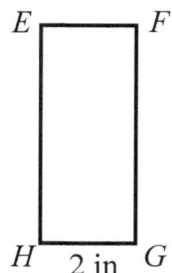

A. 0.9
B. 1.4
C. 4.7
D. 6
E. 7

40. In the parallelogram *VWXY* below, points *U*, *V*, *Y*, and *Z* form a straight line. Given that the angle measures as shown in the figure, what is the measure of angle ∠*WYX*?

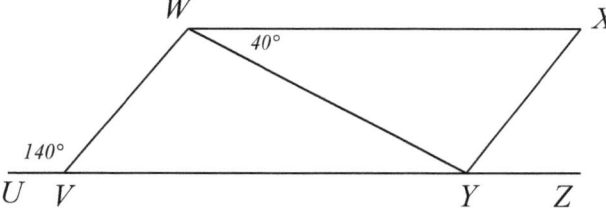

F. 25°
G. 30°
H. 40°
I. 100°
J. 140°

41. In the figure below, all interior angles are 90°, and all dimension lengths are given in centimeters. What is the perimeter of this figure, in centimeters?

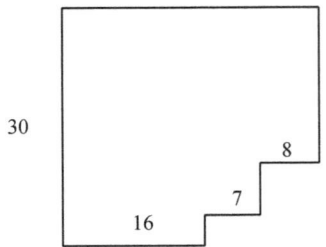

A. 30
B. 61
C. 62
D. 122
E. Cannot be determined from the given information

42. If a is a real number such that $-1 < a < 0$, which of the following numbers has the smallest value?

F. a
G. $\dfrac{1}{a}$
H. a^2
I. $\dfrac{1}{a^2}$
J. $-a^2$

43. What is $\dfrac{1}{4}$ % of 16?

A. 0.004
B. 0.04
C. 0.4
D. 4
E. 64

44. The formula $S = 20\sqrt{t + 273}$ gives the speed of sound S in meters per second near Earth's surface, where t is the surface temperature in degrees Celsius. At a point near Earth's surface, if the speed of sound is 336 meters/second, what is the corresponding temperature in degrees Celsius?

F. -20
G. 9
H. 20
I. 90
J. 200

45. Point M (-3,3) and point N (-7,5) are points on the coordinate plane. What is the length, in units, of the segment MN?

A. $\sqrt{2}$
B. $2\sqrt{2}$
C. $2\sqrt{5}$
D. 6
E. 20

46. A truck and a car are each driving along a road. The diameter of the truck's wheels are one-and-a-half times the diameter of the car's wheels. How many revolutions does one of the car's wheels make for each revolution of one of the truck's wheels?

F. $3\frac{3}{8}$
G. 3
H. $2\frac{1}{4}$
I. $1\frac{1}{2}$
J. $\frac{2}{3}$

47. Which is a point of intersection of the graphs of the equations $y = -x^2 + 6$ and $y = -0.5x^2 + 4$?

A. (3,5)
B. (0,5)
C. (2,-1)
D. (-2,2)
E. (0,3)

48. In the complex number system, $i^2 = -1$. Given that $\dfrac{5}{7-i}$ is a complex number, what is the result of $\dfrac{5}{7-i} \times \dfrac{3+i}{7+i}$?

F. $\dfrac{5}{7+i}$

G. $\dfrac{15+3i}{48}$

H. $\dfrac{10}{5+i}$

I. $\dfrac{10}{3+i}$

J. $\dfrac{3+i}{7}$

49. The figures below show regular polygons and the sum of the degrees of the angles in each polygon. Based on these figures, what is the number of degrees in a 40-sided regular polygon?

△ ▢ ⬠ ⬡
180 360 540 720

A. 2400
B. 7200
C. 6840
D. 32000
E. Cannot be determined

50. A pitcher containing 10 quarts of water was used to water 4 plants. Each plant received $\frac{1}{3}$ of the water that was remaining in the pitcher when it was watered. How many quarts of water were left in the pitcher at the time it reached the last plant?

A. $\frac{27}{64}$
B. 1
C. $1\frac{1}{26}$
D. $1\frac{11}{16}$
E. $2\frac{26}{27}$

51. If the value of $\tan \theta$ is -0.577, which of the following could be true about θ?

Note: $\tan \frac{\pi}{6} = \frac{\sqrt{3}}{3}$ and $\tan \frac{\pi}{3} = \sqrt{3}$.

A. $0 < \theta < \frac{\pi}{4}$
B. $\frac{\pi}{4} < \theta < \frac{\pi}{2}$
C. $\frac{\pi}{2} < \theta < \frac{3\pi}{4}$
D. $\frac{3\pi}{4} < \theta < \pi$
E. $\pi < \theta < \frac{5\pi}{4}$

52. If $7 + 7n$ is 40 percent bigger than k, what is k?

F. $\frac{7 + 7n}{5}$
G. $5 + 5n$
H. $2 + n$
I. $\frac{2(7 + 7n)}{5}$
J. $7 + 10n$

53. The chart below shows the percentages of the cellphone data usage by family members. The remainder of the usage will be placed in the category Not Used. If this data is to be put into a circle graph, what will be the degree measure of the Not Used wedge, rounded to the dearest degree?

FAMILY MEMBER	PERCENTAGE OF DATA
Dad	25
Mom	7
Son	21
Daughter	19

A. 28
B. 51
C. 72
D. 101
E. 259

54. If $\tan\theta = -\frac{4}{3}$, and $\pi < \theta < \frac{3\pi}{2}$, then $\sin\theta = ?$

F. $-\frac{4}{5}$
G. $-\frac{3}{4}$
H. $-\frac{3}{5}$
I. $\frac{3}{5}$
J. $\frac{4}{5}$

55. Which of the following systems of inequalities is represented by the shaded region on the coordinate plane below?

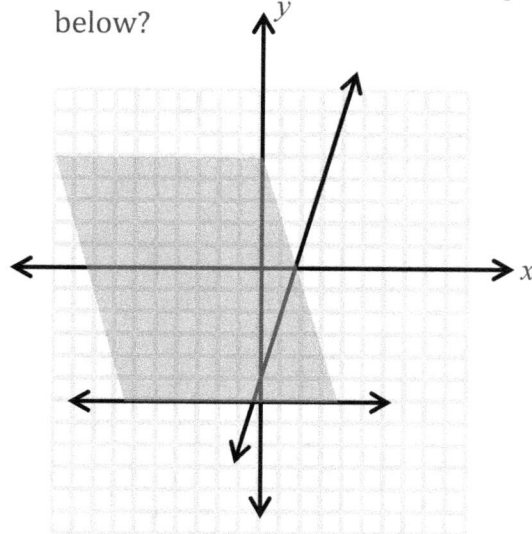

A. $y > -6$ and $y < -3x + 5$
B. $x > -6$ and $y < -3x + 5$
C. $y > -6$ and $y > -3x + 5$
D. $x > -6$ and $y > 3x + 5$
E. $y > -6$ and $y < -\frac{1}{3}x - 5$

56. If $f(x) = 2(x + 9)$ then $(x - r) = $?

F. $2x - 2r + 9$
G. $2x - r + 9$
H. $2x - r + 18$
I. $2x - 2r + 18$
J. $2(x + 9) - r$

57. Which graph below best represents the solution set for the equation
$y = 2(x+2)(x-2)$?

A.
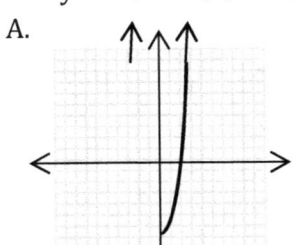

B.
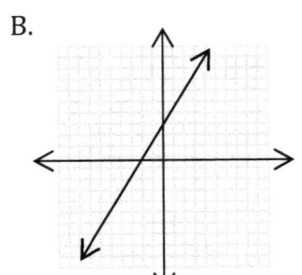

C.
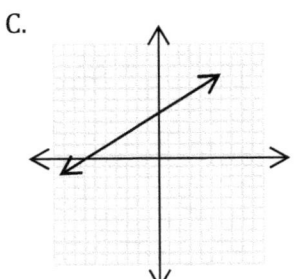

D.
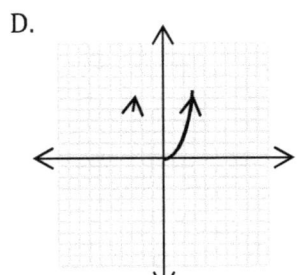

E.
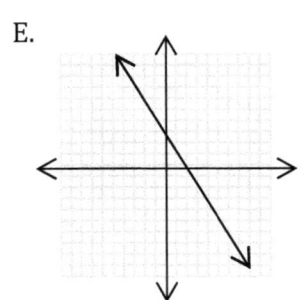

58. △PQR is reflected across the x-axis in the standard (x,y) coordinate plan. Its image is △P'Q'R', where P reflects to P'. If the coordinates of point P are (a,b), what are the coordinates of P'?

F. (b,a)
G. (-b,a)
H. (-a,-b)
I. (-a,b)
J. (a,-b)

59. If $g = 6q + 7$ and $h = 2q - 12$, what is g in terms of h?

A. $g = \dfrac{h + 12}{2}$
B. $g = \dfrac{8h + 19}{2}$
C. $3h + 43$
D. $3h + 19$
E. $h = \dfrac{g - 7}{6}$

60. Find the cos(105°) knowing that cos(105°) = cos(45°+60°). Use the formula
$cos(\alpha + \beta) = cos(\alpha)cos(\beta) - sin(\alpha)sin(\beta)$
and the table of values below.

θ	sin θ	cos θ	tan θ
30°	$\frac{1}{2}$	$\frac{\sqrt{3}}{2}$	$\frac{\sqrt{3}}{3}$
45°	$\frac{\sqrt{2}}{2}$	$\frac{\sqrt{2}}{2}$	1
60°	$\frac{\sqrt{3}}{2}$	$\frac{1}{2}$	$\sqrt{3}$

F. $\dfrac{\sqrt{2}-\sqrt{3}}{4}$

G. $\dfrac{\sqrt{6}-\sqrt{2}}{4}$

H. $\dfrac{\sqrt{2}-\sqrt{6}}{4}$

I. $\dfrac{2}{\sqrt{2}-\sqrt{6}}$

J. $\dfrac{\sqrt{2}-3}{4}$

122 | Practice Math Test Answers and Explanations

Answer Key
1. E   Story   Pre-Algebra
2. J   Concept   Algebra
3. B   Story   Pre-Algebra
4. I   Concept   Pre-Algebra
5. E   Story   Pre-Algebra
6. F   Story   Plane Geometry
7. A   Concept   Algebra
8. G   Concept   Algebra
9. B   Story   Algebra
10. G   Concept   Algebra
11. B   Diagram   Plane Geometry
12. G   Story   Pre-Algebra
13. C   Concept   Algebra
14. G   Story   Pre-Algebra
15. D   Story   Pre-Algebra
16. G   Diagram   Algebra
17. D   Concept   Coordinate Geometry
18. I   Story   Pre-Algebra
19. C   Story   Pre-Algebra
20. H   Diagram   Plane Geometry
21. D   Concept   Algebra
22. I   Concept   Intermediate Algebra
23. B   Concept   Intermediate Algebra
24. H   Diagram   Coordinate Geometry
25. A   Diagram   Plane Geometry
26. H   Story   Intermediate Algebra
27. B   Concept   Algebra
28. F   Diagram   Coordinate Geometry
29. C   Concept   Pre-Algebra
30. J   Diagram   Coordinate Geometry
31. A   Concept   Intermediate Algebra
32. H   Concept   Intermediate Algebra
33. D   Diagram   Plane Geometry
34. J   Concept   Algebra
35. E   Diagram   Coordinate Geometry
36. H   Concept   Algebra
37. D   Diagram   Plane Geometry
38. H   Diagram   Plane Geometry
39. C   Diagram   Plane Geometry
40. I   Diagram   Plane Geometry

41. D	Diagram	Plane Geometry	
42. G	Concept	Algebra	
43. B	Concept	Pre-Algebra	
44. G	Concept	Algebra	
45. C	Diagram	Coordinate Geometry	
46. I	Diagram	Plane Geometry	
47. D	Diagram	Plane Geometry	
48. H	Concept	Intermediate Algebra	
49. C	Concept	Plane Geometry	
50. E	Concept	Pre-Algebra	
51. C	Concept	Algebra	
52. G	Story	Algebra	
53. D	Story	Coordinate Geometry	
54. F	Concept	Trigonometry	
55. A	Diagram	Coordinate Geometry	
56. I	Concept	Intermediate Algebra	
57. A	Diagram	Coordinate Geometry	
58. J	Concept	Coordinate Geometry	
59. C	Concept	Intermediate Algebra	
60. H	Concept	Trigonometry	

1. **(E) – Pre-Algebra**

   To determine the total amount of fabric used, add the mixed numbers. To add mixed numbers, add the whole number parts, and then add the fractions. The whole number parts add up to 5. To add the fractions, find the least common denominator of 8 and 3, which is 24. Convert each fraction to an equivalent fraction with a denominator of 24: $\frac{5 \times 3}{8 \times 3} = \frac{15}{24}$, and $\frac{1 \times 8}{3 \times 8} = \frac{8}{24}$. Now, add the numerators, and keep the denominator: $\frac{15}{24} + \frac{8}{24} = \frac{23}{24}$. The total fabric used is $5\frac{23}{24}$.

   If you chose (B), you found a common denominator, but you did not add the numerators to get a total numerator of 5. A common error when adding fractions would result in choice (C). This fraction was obtained by the incorrect procedure of adding the numerators, and then adding the denominators.

2. **(J) – Algebra**

   To simplify the expression, first multiply the numerical coefficients to get $4 \times 6 \times 2 = 48$. To multiply the variable terms, keep the base of the variable and add the exponents. Remember that x denotes x1.
   Multiply the x variable terms: $x^3 \cdot x = x^{3+1} = x^4$. Multiply the y variable terms: $y^6 \cdot y^2 \cdot y = y^{6+2+1} = y^9$.
   The resultant expression is $48x^4y^9$.

   If your answer was (I), you fell into the common trap of multiplying the exponents instead of the correct method of adding the exponents. If your answer was either (F) or (G), you added the numerical coefficients instead of multiplying. If your answer was (H), you did not include the exponents of 1 for the single terms of x and y.

3. **(B) – Pre-Algebra**

The question is asking how many times $9.50 will go into $495. The answer will give you the number of hours needed:

$$\frac{495}{9.50} = 52.1...$$

This means that 55 hours will not be enough. Therefore, Brandy needs to work at least 56 hours.

4. **(I) – Pre-Algebra**

Method 1: Plug in

Try all the answer choices and see which one works. Choice (I), 30, does.

$5 + \sqrt{30 - 5} = 10$
$\Rightarrow 5 + \sqrt{25} = 10$
$\Rightarrow 5 + 5 = 10$ True!

Method 2: Solve
When you solve equations with radicals, start by getting all the radicals together on one side and the numbers on the other side.

$5 + \sqrt{x - 5} = 10$
$\Rightarrow \sqrt{x - 5} = 5$
$\Rightarrow x - 5 = 25$ (squaring both sides)
$\Rightarrow x = 30$

5. **(E) – Pre-Algebra**

Since 1 cup of the substance weighs 8.32 grams, there are $\frac{460}{8.32}$ cups in the container.

$$\frac{460}{8.32} = 55.288$$

You now want to find how many times $1\frac{3}{5}$ cups will go into 55.288 cups.

Use your calculator to find $\frac{55.288}{1.6}$. The answer is 34.555..., which

means 34 full units.

6. **(F) – Plane Geometry**

   If $\frac{1}{4}$ inch represents 60 feet, 1 inch represents 240 feet.

   $$\frac{240}{1} = \frac{80}{x} \Rightarrow x = \frac{80}{240} = \frac{1}{3}$$

7. **(A) – Algebra**

   Don't forget to cube every factor in parentheses:

   $(6x)^3 = 6^3 x^3 = 216x^3$
   $\therefore 4x \cdot (6x)^3 = (4x)(216x^3) = 864x^4$

8. **(G) – Algebra**

   This is an equation with a variable on both sides. To solve, work to get the n terms isolated on one side of the equation, and the numerical terms on the other side. Subtract 4n from both sides to get 9n – 4n – 6 = 4n – 4n + 26. Combine like terms: 5n – 6 = 26. Now add 6 to both sides: 5n – 6 + 6 = 26 + 6, or 5n = 32. Finally, divide both sides by 5: $n = \frac{32}{5}$.

   Answer choice (F) reflects a common trap: forgetting to divide by 5. If you chose answer choice (H) or (I), you incorrectly added 9n and 4n, and possibly subtracted 6 from 26 instead of adding 6. Dividing incorrectly at the last step would have led you to answer choice (J).

9. **(B) – Algebra**

   For the first bean, $P(\text{white}) = \frac{5}{8}$.

   For the second bean, $P(\text{white}) = \frac{4}{7}$

Both events must happen:

$$P(\text{white, white}) = \frac{5}{8} \cdot \frac{4}{7} = \frac{20}{56}$$

10. (G) – Algebra

First, solve the equation $5m^2 = 45$ for m. once a value is obtained for m, substitute this into the expression to evaluate and find the answer. To solve the equation, divide both sides of the equation by 5 to get $m^2 = 9$. Take the square root of each side to get m = 3, or m = -3. Now, evaluate the expression. Because the expression contains the radical $\sqrt{3m}$, and the expression must be a real number, reject the value of m = -3. When a radicand, the expression under the radical sign, is negative, the number does not have a value in the set of real numbers. Substitute 3 for m in the expression: $3^2 + \sqrt{3(3)} = 9 + \sqrt{9} = 9 + 3 = 12$.

11. (B) – Plane Geometry

The circle is inscribed,

∴ BDC is tangent to the circle at D.

∴ $\angle EDC$ is a right angle (tangent-radius theorem).

Also, $\angle B$ is a right angle (given).

Both triangles ABC and EDC contain $\angle C$.

∴ $\triangle ABC$ is similar to $\triangle EDC$ (angle-angle similarity)

∴ $\dfrac{AB}{BC} = \dfrac{ED}{DC}$

∴ $\dfrac{5}{6} = \dfrac{ED}{4}$

$\Rightarrow ED = \dfrac{20}{6} = 3\dfrac{1}{3}$

12. (G) – Pre-Algebra

Probability is a ratio that compares the number of favorable, or

desired, outcomes to the total number of outcomes. Probability is always a number between 0 and 1, and is never greater than 1. In this question, the favorable outcome is the number of options that are NOT green, or 7 + 8 = 15. The total number of outcomes is 10 + 7 + 8 = 25. The probability that it is NOT green is $\frac{15}{25} = \frac{3}{5}$, in lowest terms. Choice (F) is the probability that it IS green. Choice (H) is the ratio that compares green to other colors.

13. (C) – Algebra

A 2 × 3 matrix multiplied by a 3 × 2 matrix gives a 2 × 2 matrix as the result.

To get the first-row, first column value of the answer, multiply the first row of the first matrix by the first column of the second matrix.

To get the first-row, second-column value of the answer, multiply the first row of the first matrix by the second column of the second matrix, and so on.

For the given matrices:

$$\begin{bmatrix} 2 & 6 & 3 \\ 5 & 0 & 4 \end{bmatrix} \begin{bmatrix} 2 & 1 \\ -3 & 4 \\ 1 & -2 \end{bmatrix}$$

$$= \begin{bmatrix} (2)(2) + (6)(-3) + (3)(1) & (2)(1) + (6)(4) + (3)(-2) \\ (5)(2) + (0)(-3) + (4)(1) & (5)(1) + (0)(4) + (4)(-2) \end{bmatrix}$$

$$= \begin{bmatrix} -11 & 20 \\ 14 & -3 \end{bmatrix}$$

14. (G) – Pre-Algebra

To find an average, calculate the sum of the data and then divide by the total number of data items. According to the table, the number of hours that the Country genre has a "live" disc jockey is 6, 3, and 12. 6 + 3 + 12 = 21. Divide: 21 ÷ 3 = 7

Answer choice (F) is the number of *entries*, not hours, for the Country genre. Choice (I) is the average number of hours for the Classical genre. Answer choice (J) is the average number of hours for the News genre.

15. **(D) - Pre-Algebra**

    This problem tests your ability to read a table of information. You must study the wording in the problem and study the table to understand its structure. To determine the minimum number of disc jockeys needed given the information in the problem, add up all of the hours (the last column) and then divide by 9 (the number of hours a disc jockey works). From the table, the number of hours is: 6 + 3 + 12 + 24 + 7 + 16 + 24 + 24 + 24 + 14 + 5 + 12 + 24 = 195 total hours. 195 ÷ 9 = 21.66, which means you must have 22 disc jockeys, because you cannot have a fraction of a person.

    A common trap would be answer choice (C), because the answer would round down to 24 disc jockeys, but this would fall short of the requirement to fulfill all of the hours.

    Choice (E) reflects the total number of hours needed. Answer choice (A) is the number of 24-hour segments that require a "live" disc jockey.

16. **(G) – Algebra:**

    To find the missing value, add the monomials in the first row: 2m + -8m + 6m = 0. This first row sums to zero. To be sure, check the rightmost column: 6m + -4m + -2m = 0. Every row, column, and diagonal must sum to 0. The first column must therefore be 2m + 4m + □ = 0, or 6m + □ = 0. Isolate the missing term on one side of the equation by subtracting 6m from both sides: □ = -6m.

If your choice was (H), you ignored the m variable in the term. If your choice was (F), (I), or (J), you may have just looked at the first column and the last row and found a value that would work with those, without considering the other rows, columns, and diagonals.

17. (D) – Coordinate Geometry

The algebraic expression xy means to multiply the point's x value by its y value. If the product is positive, then the x and y factors are either both positive or both negative, according to the rules for multiplying signed numbers. Positive x-coordinates are to the right of the origin. Positive y-coordinates are above the origin. In quadrant I, both coordinates are positive, and in quadrant III, both coordinates are negative. In quadrant II, the x-coordinate is negative (to the left of the origin) and the y-coordinate is positive (above the origin). In quadrant IV, the x-coordinate is positive (to the right of the origin), and y-coordinate is negative (below the origin).

18. (I) – Pre-Algebra

Work backward from the answer choices, and see which one leaves Mark with $12. Choice (F), $120, leaves Mark with $24, double what you want. This suggests that choice (I), $60, may work. Try it next.

$\frac{1}{5}$ of $60 = $12, which leaves $48.

$\frac{1}{4}$ of $48 = $12, which leaves $36.

$\frac{1}{3}$ of $36 = $12, which leaves $24.

$\frac{1}{2}$ of $24 = $12, which leaves $12, which was required.

19. **(C) – Pre-Algebra**

Total length of movie = 135 mins.

Total minutes for commercials = 45 mins.

As a percent: $\frac{45}{135} \times \frac{100}{1} = 33\%$

20. **(H) – Plane Geometry**

Draw a diagram of a rectangle:

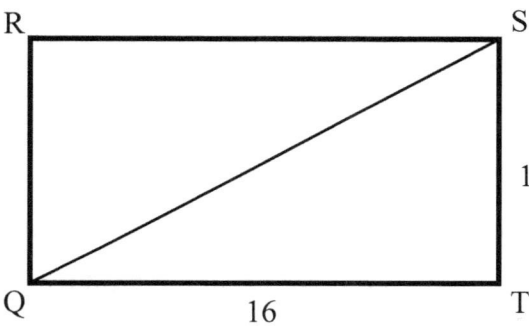

Because a rectangle has 4 right angles, you can treat the diagonal, QS, as the hypotenuse of a right triangle with legs of 12 and 16 inches. Use the Pythagorean theorem to solve for the length of the hypotenuse. If c represents the length of the hypotenuse and a and b represent the length of the legs, then $a^2 + b^2 = c^2$. Substitute into the formula:

$c^2 = 12^2 + 16^2$

$c^2 = 144 + 256$

$c^2 = 100$

Take the square root of both sides of the equation to find that c = 20 inches.

21. (D) – Algebra

Factor and cancel:

$$\frac{3x^2 - 3x - 18}{3x^2 - 27} = \frac{3(x^2 - x - 6)}{3(x^2 - 9)} = \frac{3(x-3)(x+2)}{3(x-3)(x+3)} = \frac{x+2}{x+3}$$

22. (I) – Intermediate Algebra

Each of the answer choices is in the form "y = ...", so solve for y in terms of x. isolate y on one side of the equation. First, subtract 3x from both sides: 3x – 3x + 2y = -3x + 18. Combine like terms to get 2y = -3x + 18. Now, divide all terms on both sides by 2: y = $-2^{\frac{3}{2}x}$ + 9.

In answer choice (F) the numeric term 18 is not divided by 2. Answer choices (G) and (J) have the reciprocal of the coefficient of x. In answer choice (H), 3x was added to both sides of the equation instead of subtracted, to get the incorrect term of $+2^{\frac{3}{2}x}$.

23. (B) – Intermediate Algebra

Sum of roots = -5 means $-\frac{b}{a} = -5 \Rightarrow b = 5a$

Product of roots = 4 means $\frac{c}{a} = 4 \Rightarrow c = 4a$

Notice that these relationships are true only in choice (B), where $a=1$, $b=3$, and $c=5$.

24. (H) – Coordinate Geometry

The sine (sin) ratio is the ratio of the side opposite to angle Q, to the hypotenuse of the right angle. The sin Q = $\frac{12}{13}$.

25. (A) – Plane Geometry

Since QRTU is still a parallelogram QU = RT. Therefore QU =12.

26. (H) – Intermediate Algebra

For the first 5 GB: (5)(2)=$10.

For the next 10 GB: (10)(4)=$40.

For the remaining 25 GB: (25)(5)=$125.

Total= $175.

27. (B) – Algebra

For any angle α, the range of $\cos \alpha$ is $-1 \leq \cos \alpha \leq 1$.

When you multiply by 3, the inequality becomes $-3 \leq 3 \cos \alpha \leq 3$.

Notice that the size of α does not matter – whether it is 3θ, or 4θ, or 100θ.

The minimum value of the expression is -3.

28. (F) – Coordinate Geometry

The tangent is the ratio of the side opposite to the given angle over the side adjacent to the given angle. Segment EF is the side opposite to the angle D, so call this side m. Segment DE, the adjacent side to angle D, equals 38 inches. Set up the equation:

$$\frac{7}{8} = \frac{m}{38}$$

(38)(7) = 8m

266 = 8m

m = 33.25

If you chose (G), you added 38 and $\frac{7}{8}$. Answer choice (H) reflects the length of side DF, the hypotenuse of the right angle.

29. (C) – Pre-Algebra

To find the average of three numbers, even if they're algebraic expression, add them and divide by 3.

$$Average = \frac{Sum\ of\ terms}{number\ of\ terms}$$

$$= \frac{(5x-12)+(3x-7)+(-2x+17)}{3}$$

$$= \frac{6x-2}{3}$$

$$= 2x - \frac{2}{3}$$

30. (J) Coordinate Geometry

Let $BC = x$. Then $AB = 2x$. You are given that $AB + BC + CD = 24$.

∴ $2x + x + CD = 24$, which implies that $CD = 24 - 3x$

Notice that if $CD = 24$, $x = BC = 0$, which is not consistent with the information given in the problem. (The lengths must be positive.) Therefore, CD cannot be 24.

31. (A) – Intermediate Algebra

You are given:

$2x+2y=16$

$x+2z=25$

$y+z=13$

The arithmetic mean of x, y and z equals $\frac{x+y+z}{3}$. So a good place to start might be to add the three equations and see where that takes you. Adding the left sides of setting that equal to the sum of the right sides leaves you with: $3x + 3y + 3z = 54$. Dividing by 3 gives you the sum of $x, y,$ and z that you want: $x + y + z = 18$. Thus, the average of the

Practice Math Test Answers and Explanations | 135

three numbers is $\frac{18}{3} = 6$.

32. (H) – Intermediate Algebra

To solve, you need to eliminate the i in the denominator by multiplying the given fraction by $\frac{i}{i}$.

$$\frac{i+2}{i} = \frac{i+2}{i} \cdot \frac{i}{i} = \frac{i^2 + 2i}{i^2} = \frac{-1+2i}{-1} = 1 - 2i$$

33. (D) – Plane Geometry

The area of a parallelogram is A = bh, where height is the h is the length of the perpendicular segment to one of the sides of the parallelogram. In the figure, segment RT, of length 8 + 5, or 13 mm, is the base and the dotted segment, of length 12 mm, is the height. The area is 13 x 12 = 156 mm².

Answer choice (A) is the area of the little triangle at the top, not the parallelogram. If you chose answer choice (B), you added the given numbers, without recognizing that the problem is asking for area. Answer choice (C) is the perimeter of the parallelogram. Answer (E) reflects a common error, where you multiplied the sides together, instead of the base times the height.

34. (J) – Algebra

$f(x) = f(-x)$ for any function whose powers of x are all even. A quick glance at the answer choices shows that choice (J) is the only function with this feature. If you did not figure this out, you can get the answer by substituting simple numerical values into the functions given. For example, try $x=1$. The function is choice (J) is the only one in which $f(1) = f(-1)$:

$f(1) = -1 + 7 = 6$

$f(-1) = (-1)^4 + 7 = -1 + 7 = 6$

35. (E) – Coordinate Geometry

Because all streets and avenues shown intersect at right angles, the map is a rectangle in which opposite sides have the same measures. To find the location half way from C and S, first think of the corner of Gold and 10th to be the origin, or (0,0). Just as in coordinate geometry, the first ordered pair represents the east-west direction and the second ordered pair represents the north-south direction. The distance from the origin at Gold Street to the school is 4 miles east. The distance from the origin at 10th Avenue to the convention center is 8 miles north. The new station will be halfway between these coordinates, or $\frac{4}{2} = 2$ miles east of the origin and $\frac{8}{2} = 4$ miles north of the origin. To drive from G to the new grocery store, you would have to drive 6 – 2 = 4 miles west on Main Street, and then 10 – 4 = 6 miles south on Elm Street (the first two miles south to get to 3rd Avenue, and then the 4 more miles south to be halfway from the convention center and the school).

Choice A is the directions of the new grocery store starting from the origin at Gold and 10th. Choice (B) is the directions of the new grocery store starting from the school. Choice (C) is the direction from the corner of Main and Gold to the new station. If you answered choice (D), you forgot to add in the 2 miles on Coal Street to get from Main to 3rd Avenue.

36. (H) – Algebra

$$\frac{x - 4y}{5y} = \frac{60}{100} = \frac{3}{5}$$

$$\Rightarrow 5x - 20y = 15y$$

$$\Rightarrow 5x = 35y$$

$$\Rightarrow \frac{x}{y} = \frac{35}{5} = 7$$

37. (D) – Plane Geometry

Sketch a diagram.

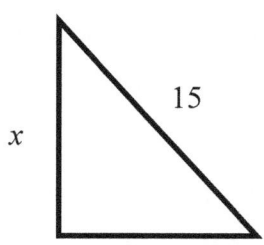

Use the Pythagorean Theorem to solve for x.

$$15^2 = 9^2 + x^2$$

$$x^2 = 15^2 - 9^2$$

$$x = \sqrt{225 - 81}$$

$$x = \sqrt{144} = 12$$

38. (H) – Plane Geometry

The area of a circle is $A = \pi r^2$, where r is the radius of the circle. Use the equation $25\pi = \pi r^2$ and solve for r by dividing both sides by π: $25 = r^2$. If you take the square root of both sides then r = 5 or -5. Reject the -5 value, because a radius length cannot be negative. The radius of the circle is 5, so the diameter of the circle, which is the same as the length of a side of the square, is 2 x 5 = 10 units.

Answer choice (F) is the area of the square. Choice (G) is r^2. Choosing choice (I) is a common error that mistakes the radius of the circle for the side of the square.

39. (C) – Algebra

When figures are similar, the side lengths are in proportion Let x represent the missing side length and set up the proportion of shorter side to longer side: $\frac{3}{7} = \frac{2}{x}$. Cross-multiply to get 3x – 14. Divide both sides by 3 to get x = 14 ÷ 3 = 4.7, to the nearest tenth of an inch.

If you chose answer choice (A), you set up the proportion incorrectly – make sure to match up the long sides and the short sides on the same side of the fraction. Answer choice (D) is the most common error make with similar figures, by assuming that since 3 – 1 = 2 that the missing side would be 7 – 1 = 6. Similar figures have sides that are in proportion, which is not an additive relationship.

40. (I) – Plane Geometry

The figure shown is a parallelogram. Extend the top side out to make a parallel line to line UZ. Line WY is a transversal to the parallel lines, forming alternate interior angles, ∠XWY and ∠WYV, which have the same measures of 40°. Line WV is another transversal line to the parallel lines, forming alternate interior angles, ∠UVW and ∠VWX. Because they have the same measure, ∠VWX = 140°. In addition, ∠VWX and ∠VYX have the same measure – they are opposite angles in a parallelogram. Now, ∠VYZ - ∠WYV - ∠WYX, or 140 – 40 = 100°.

If your answer was choice (H), you incorrectly thought that ∠WYX had the same measure as ∠XWY. Answer choice (J) is the measure of ∠VYX, not ∠WYX.

41. (D) – Plane Geometry

The key to solving this problem is to simplify the drawing, knowing that you are looking for the perimeter. This figure, for perimeter purposes, can be thought of as a rectangle – just "lower" all the bottom pieces and move all left pieces to the right and you have a rectangle, with side lengths of 30 centimeters, and top/bottom lengths of 16 + 7 + 5 = 31 centimeters.

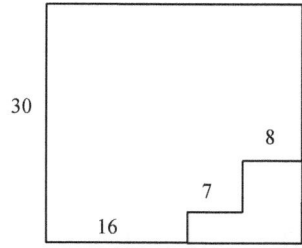

The perimeter is two times the length plus two times the width, or 2(30) + 2(31) = 60 + 62 = 122 centimeters.

Choice (A) is the measure of the length. Choice (B) is just the measure of two sides of the figure (just the numbers that are shown).

42. (G) – Algebra

Use the pick-a-number strategy. Pick a number that lies between -1 and 0, for example $-\frac{1}{3}$. Comparing values is now very easy:

Choice (F): $a = -\frac{1}{3}$

Choice (G): $\frac{1}{a} = -3$

Choice (H): $a^2 = \frac{1}{9}$

Choice (J): $\frac{1}{a^2} = 9$

Choice (K): $-a^2 = -\frac{1}{9}$

Of these, -3 is the smallest. Therefore, $\frac{1}{a}$ has the smallest value.

43. (B) – Pre-Algebra

Be careful. The question is not asking for $\frac{1}{4}$ of 16. It's asking for $\frac{1}{4}$ % of 16. One-fourth of 1 percent is 0.25%, or 0.0025:

$\frac{1}{4}$ % of 16 = 0.0025 x 16 = 0.04

44. (G) – Pre-Algebra

Method 1: Plug in

You want to find the value of t such that $336 = 20\sqrt{t + 273}$ or, more simply, $16.8 = \sqrt{t + 273}$.

You should be able to get the answer quickly by plugging in the answer choices and estimating which value of t gives the answer closest to 16.8.

If $t = -20$, $\sqrt{253} \approx 15.9$ (too small)

If $t = 9$, $\sqrt{282} \approx 16.8$ (looks good). Therefore t is 9.

Notice that $t = 20$ gives answer that is too high.

Method 2: Solve the equation

This is a problem where the given equation is easy enough for you and your calculator to find a quick solution!

$336 = 20\sqrt{t + 273}$

$\Rightarrow 16.8 = \sqrt{t + 273}$

$\Rightarrow 282.24 = t + 273$ (squaring both sides)

$\Rightarrow t = 9.24$

$\Rightarrow t \approx 9$

Practice Math Test Answers and Explanations | 141

45. (C) – Coordinate Geometry

To find the length of segment MN, use the distance formula: $d = \sqrt{(x_2 - x_1)^2 + (y_2 - y_1)^2}$. Substitute in the point values:

$$d = \sqrt{(-7 - (-3))^2 + (5 - 3)^2}$$
$$d = \sqrt{4^2 + 2^2}$$
$$d = \sqrt{20} = \sqrt{4} \times \sqrt{5} + 2\sqrt{5}$$

46. (I) – Plane Geometry

The ratio $\dfrac{Truck\ wheel\ diameter}{Car\ wheel\ diameter} = \dfrac{3}{2}$ describes the difference between the wheels.

In order to solve the problem, we must find the ratio $\dfrac{circumference\ of\ truck\ wheel}{circumference\ of\ car\ wheel}$.

Recall these facts: For two circles, if the ratio of their radii is $\dfrac{r_1}{r_2}$, then the ratio of their diameter is $\dfrac{r_1}{r_2}$, the ratio of their circumference is $\dfrac{r_1}{r_2}$, and the ratio of their areas is $\left(\dfrac{r_1}{r_2}\right)^2$.

$\therefore \dfrac{C_1}{C_2} = \dfrac{r_1}{r_2} = \dfrac{3}{2}$. This means that the smaller wheel makes 1.5 revolutions for every revolution of the larger wheel.

47. (D) – Plane Geometry

Use the plug-in technique. Remember, the ordered pair that works must satisfy *both* equations. Choice (A), (B), (C), and (E) are very easy to eliminate:

Choice (A): (3, 5) does not work in the first equation.
Choice (B): (0, 5) does not work in the second equation.

Choice (C): (2, -1) does not work in the first equation.

Choice (E): (0, 3) does not work in the first equation.

Choice (D), however, works in both:

$2 = -(-2)^2 + 6$

$2 = -\frac{1}{2}(-2)^2 + 4$

48. (H) – Intermediate Algebra

In the complex number system, i^2 is defined to be equal to -1, as you are told in the question prompt. Use the distributive property to multiply the fraction:

$$\frac{5}{7-i} \times \frac{3+i}{7+i} = \frac{(5 \times 3) + 5i}{7^2 + 7i - 7i - i^2} = \frac{15 + 5i}{49 - (-1)} = \frac{15 + 5i}{50} = \frac{3+i}{10}$$

49. (C) – Plane Geometry

One way to solve this problem is to make a table. Each time the number of sides goes up by 1, the sum of the angles goes up by 180°. Make a third column in the table to discover a relationship.

Number of Sides	Sum of the Angles	
3	180°	180° x 1
4	360°	180° x 2
5	540°	180° x 3
6	720°	180° x 4

Notice that to find the sum of the angles, you can multiply 180 times 2 less than the number of sides of the polygon. Multiply 180(40-2) to get 6840. This is choice (C).

If you chose choice (A), you may have just considered the triangle, and assumed that the relationship was 60 times the number of sides. If your answer was choice (B), you may have noticed that the number of degrees rose by 180°, but did not consider the sides of the polygons. Choice (D) is a relationship that works for the 3-sided and 6-sided polygons, but not for the other two.

50. (E) - Pre-Algebra

The amount of water left at each stage is $\frac{2}{3}$ of the previous amount. The numbers representing how much water is left are shown in the following sequence:

After plant 1, after plant 2, after plant 3, …

$10\left(\frac{2}{3}\right)$, $10\left(\frac{2}{3}\right)^2$, $10\left(\frac{2}{3}\right)^3$,   …

The amount left after plant 3 is what is required.

$10\left(\frac{2}{3}\right)^3 = 10\left(\frac{2^3}{3^3}\right) = \frac{80}{27} = 2\frac{26}{27}$ quarts left

51. (C) – Algebra

Because the value of $\tan \theta$ is negative, θ cannot be in either Quadrant 1 or III. Therefore, you should eliminate choices (A), (B), and (E). The only possibilities are choices (C) and (D), both of which place θ in Quadrant II. Since $y = \tan x$ is an increasing function, $\tan \frac{\pi}{3} > \tan \frac{\pi}{6}$. (You can also see this from the given note.) Use the inverse tan function, $\tan^{-1}$, to find an angle whose tan is 0.577. The calculator will give you a reference angle close to $30°$. This tells you that the angle, θ, is approximately $150°$ and lies between $\frac{3\pi}{4}(135°)$ and $\pi(180°)$.

52. (G) - Algebra

This $7 + 7n$ is 40% bigger than k.

$$\Rightarrow 7 + 7n = \left(k + \frac{2}{5}k\right) = \frac{7}{5}k.$$

$$\Rightarrow k = \frac{5(7+7n)}{7}$$

$$= 5 + 5n$$

53. (D) – Coordinate Geometry

First, determine the percentage in the category Not Used. The total percentage must sum to 100%, so the percentage for Not Used is 100 − 25 − 7 − 21 − 19 = 28%. To find the number of degrees in a circle graph that corresponds with 28%, set up the ratio, where x represents the number of degrees for the Not Used category. Recall that there are 360° in a circle: $\frac{28}{100} = \frac{x}{360}$. Cross multiply to get 28 x 360 = 100x, or 10,080 = 100x. Divide both sides by 100 to get x = 101°, rounded to the nearest degree.

Choice (A) is a common trap that represents the percentage, not the number of degrees in a circle graph. If your answer was choice (B), you thought that there were 180° in a circle. Answer choice (C) is the percentage of categories that are not in Not Used, and choice (E) is the number of degrees that are not in Not Used.

54. (F) – Trigonometry

The information that $\pi < \theta < \frac{3\pi}{2}$ tells you that the angle is in quadrant III of the coordinate plane, in quadrant III, the sin values are negative. So the answer must be negative. Eliminate (I), and (J). You are given the value of tan θ, which is the ratio of the opposite side to the adjacent side of a right triangle. Sketch this triangle, using leg lengths of 4 and 3:

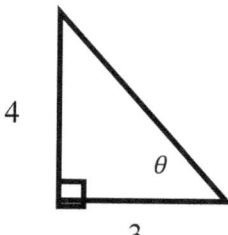

This is a special right triangle, the 3-4-5 Pythagorean triple, so the hypotenuse is 5 units in length. The sin of an angle is the ratio of the length of the opposite side to the length of the hypotenuse, or $\frac{4}{5}$.

Choice (G) is the cotangent of the angle. Choices (H) and (I) are cosine values for the angle for quadrants II and I, respectively. If you chose choice (J), you may have ignored the fact that the angle is in quadrant III, and thought that the sin value would be positive.

55. (A) – Coordinate Geometry

Look at the graphed boundary lines for the inequalities. Find the equation for these boundary lines and then determine if the shading represents less than or greater than these boundary lines. The horizontal line has a slope of 0 and a y-intercept (where the line crosses the y-axis) of -6, so the equation of this boundary line is y = -6. It is shaded above this line, so the inequality is y > -6. The slanted line has a slope with a change in y values of -3 and a change in x values of 1, so the slope is $-\frac{3}{1} = -3$. The y-intercept is 5. The line is decreasing, so the slope is negative. The shading is less than, or below, this boundary line, so the inequality is y < -3x + 5.

If you chose answer choice (B), you fell into a common trap of interpreting the horizontal boundary line equation to be x > -6. Answer choice (C) is another common error, thinking that the shading represents more than, or above, the slanted line. Answer choice (D) interprets the slope as 3. Positive slopes increases, or slants upwards, when going from left to right. Answer choice (E) represents a slope of $-\frac{1}{3}$, not the correct slope of -3. A slope of $-\frac{1}{3}$ would mean for every change of 1 in the y values, the x values would change by -3.

56. (I) – Intermediate Algebra

The question asks you to evaluate the function f(x), replacing x with (x - r). Replace any instance of x in the function definition with x - r: 2(x + 9) will be 2(x - r + 9). Use the distributive property and multiply each term in parentheses by 2 to get 2x – 2r + 2 x 9, or 2x – 2r + 18.

In choice (F), the 2 was not distributed to the constant term 9. Choice (G) only multiplies the 2 by the first tem in the parentheses. In choices (H) and (J), the c term was just added onto the end of the function definition, instead of replacing the x with (x - r).

Practice Math Test Answers and Explanations | 147

57. (A) – Coordinate Geometry

Convert the equation to slope-intercept form.

$y = 2(x + 2)(x - 2) = 2(x^2 - 4) = 2x^2 - 8$

This is the graph of answer A.

58. (J) - Coordinate Geometry

This In general, when a point is reflected across the x-axis, the image keeps the same x-coordinate but the y-coordinate changes sign.

59. (C) – Intermediate Algebra

The problem is asking what is the value of g in terms of h. The two given equations do not show a direct relationship between g and h, so you must solve for q in the second equation to get q in terms of h, and then substitute this value in for q in the first equation. To solve for q in the second equation, isolate q by first adding 12 to both sides of the equation: h + 12 = 2q – 12 + 12, or h + 12 = 2q. Divide both sides by 2 to get $\frac{h+12}{2}$ = q. use this value of q in the first equation: g = 6q + 3 becomes g = $\frac{6(h+12)}{2}$ + 7. Factor out a 2 from the numerator and the denominator to get g = 3(h + 12) + 7. Multiply the terms in parentheses by 3, or g = 3h + 36 + 7, or g = 3h + 43.

Answer choice (A) is the value of q in terms of h, from the second equation. In choice (B) the constant term 7 in the first equation was incorrectly added to the numerator of the transformed first equation. In answer choice (D), the 2 was factored out correctly, but the remaining 3 was not distributed to the constant term of 12. Choice (E) is the value of q, not h, in terms of g from the first equation.

60. (H) – Trigonometry

In this problem, you are asked to use the formula $\cos(\alpha + \beta) = \cos(\alpha)\cos(\beta) - \sin(\alpha)\sin(\beta)$ and the table of values, to find the value of $\cos(105°) = \cos(45° + 60°)$. Substitute in 45° for α and 60° for β to get: $\cos(45°)\cos(60°) - \sin(45°)\sin(60°)$. Now, use the table to replace each sin or cos with the corresponding values in the table:

$$\frac{\sqrt{2}}{2} \times \frac{1}{2} - \frac{\sqrt{2}}{2} \times \frac{\sqrt{3}}{2}$$

Using order of operations, multiply and then add the numerators and keep the denominator:

$$\frac{\sqrt{2}}{4} - \frac{\sqrt{6}}{4} = \frac{\sqrt{2} - \sqrt{6}}{4}$$

Alternatively, you could use your calculator to find the value of the $\cos(105°) = -0.2588$, and then test each answer choice to find the answer closest to this value. Choice (H) will be the only value to equal the $\cos(105°)$.

If you chose answer choice (F) or choice (J), you probably used the wrong values in the table. In answer choice (G), you forgot that the $\cos(105°)$ will be a negative number. Answer choice (I) is a common trap – you correctly used the table, but did not multiply the denominators to get a denominator of 4.

Troubleshooting Math Tactics

For each question you missed, find the reason in the left column and write the question number in the adjacent right column.

Time? *I did not:*	Question Number	The Question? *I did not:*	Question Number	The Answer? *I did not:*	Question Number
• Make two passes		• Ignore insignificant issues		• Recognize the answer was in a different format from the question	
• Use all of my time		• Put question in an understandable format		• Eliminated and guessed or guessed incorrectly	
• Spend 45 minutes on the first pass and 15 minutes on the second pass		• Grasp, Evaluate, Elect (**GEE**)		• Recognize insignificant issues in the answer choices	
• Identify the difficult or impossible questions, or spent too much time on them during the first pass		• Replace variables with numbers		• Understand the meaning of important words	
• Slash the bubbles		• Guesstimate		• Made a computation error	
• Stay on the grid		• Eyeball diagrams			
		• Backsolve			
		• Use Q. S. NRAF for story problems			

For each question missed, record the subject and type of question. Write the number of the missed question in each of the categories.

Subject						Type		
Prealgebra	Elementary Algebra	Intermediate Algebra	Coordinate Geometry	Plane Geometry	Trigonometry	Diagram	Story	Concept

Troubleshooting Math Tactics

For each question you missed, find the reason in the left column and write the question number in the adjacent right column.

Time? *I did not:*	Question Number	The Question? *I did not:*	Question Number	The Answer? *I did not:*	Question Number
• Make two passes		• Ignore insignificant issues		• Recognize the answer was in a different format from the question	
• Use all of my time		• Put question in an understandable format		• Eliminated and guessed or guessed incorrectly	
• Spend 45 minutes on the first pass and 15 minutes on the second pass		• Grasp, Evaluate, Elect (**GEE**)		• Recognize insignificant issues in the answer choices	
• Identify the difficult or impossible questions, or spent too much time on them during the first pass		• Replace variables with numbers		• Understand the meaning of important words	
• Slash the bubbles		• Guesstimate		• Made a computation error	
• Stay on the grid		• Eyeball diagrams			
		• Backsolve			
		• Use Q. S. NRAF for story problems			

For each question missed, record the subject and type of question. Write the number of the missed question in each of the categories.

Subject						Type		
Prealgebra	Elementary Algebra	Intermediate Algebra	Coordinate Geometry	Plane Geometry	Trigonometry	Diagram	Story	Concept

Troubleshooting Math Tactics

For each question you missed, find the reason in the left column and write the question number in the adjacent right column.

Time? *I did not:*	Question Number	The Question? *I did not:*	Question Number	The Answer? *I did not:*	Question Number
• Make two passes		• Ignore insignificant issues		• Recognize the answer was in a different format from the question	
• Use all of my time		• Put question in an understandable format		• Eliminated and guessed or guessed incorrectly	
• Spend 45 minutes on the first pass and 15 minutes on the second pass		• Grasp, Evaluate, Elect (**GEE**)		• Recognize insignificant issues in the answer choices	
• Identify the difficult or impossible questions, or spent too much time on them during the first pass		• Replace variables with numbers		• Understand the meaning of important words	
• Slash the bubbles		• Guesstimate		• Made a computation error	
• Stay on the grid		• Eyeball diagrams			
		• Backsolve			
		• Use Q. S. NRAF for story problems			

For each question missed, record the subject and type of question. Write the number of the missed question in each of the categories.

Subject						Type		
Prealgebra	Elementary Algebra	Intermediate Algebra	Coordinate Geometry	Plane Geometry	Trigonometry	Diagram	Story	Concept

Troubleshooting Math Tactics

For each question you missed, find the reason in the left column and write the question number in the adjacent right column.

Time? I did not:	Question Number	The Question? I did not:	Question Number	The Answer? I did not:	Question Number
• Make two passes		• Ignore insignificant issues		• Recognize the answer was in a different format from the question	
• Use all of my time		• Put question in an understandable format		• Eliminated and guessed or guessed incorrectly	
• Spend 45 minutes on the first pass and 15 minutes on the second pass		• Grasp, Evaluate, Elect (**GEE**)		• Recognize insignificant issues in the answer choices	
• Identify the difficult or impossible questions, or spent too much time on them during the first pass		• Replace variables with numbers		• Understand the meaning of important words	
• Slash the bubbles		• Guesstimate		• Made a computation error	
• Stay on the grid		• Eyeball diagrams			
		• Backsolve			
		• Use Q. S. NRAF for story problems			

For each question missed, record the subject and type of question. Write the number of the missed question in each of the categories.

Subject						Type		
Prealgebra	Elementary Algebra	Intermediate Algebra	Coordinate Geometry	Plane Geometry	Trigonometry	Diagram	Story	Concept

Troubleshooting Math Tactics

For each question you missed, find the reason in the left column and write the question number in the adjacent right column.

Time? *I did not:*	Question Number	The Question? *I did not:*	Question Number	The Answer? *I did not:*	Question Number
• Make two passes		• Ignore insignificant issues		• Recognize the answer was in a different format from the question	
• Use all of my time		• Put question in an understandable format		• Eliminated and guessed or guessed incorrectly	
• Spend 45 minutes on the first pass and 15 minutes on the second pass		• Grasp, Evaluate, Elect (**GEE**)		• Recognize insignificant issues in the answer choices	
• Identify the difficult or impossible questions, or spent too much time on them during the first pass		• Replace variables with numbers		• Understand the meaning of important words	
• Slash the bubbles		• Guesstimate		• Made a computation error	
• Stay on the grid		• Eyeball diagrams			
		• Backsolve			
		• Use Q. S. NRAF for story problems			

For each question missed, record the subject and type of question. Write the number of the missed question in each of the categories.

Subject						Type		
Prealgebra	Elementary Algebra	Intermediate Algebra	Coordinate Geometry	Plane Geometry	Trigonometry	Diagram	Story	Concept

Quick Facts

• For the Writing test, you will have 30 minutes to complete one essay that measures your writing skills.

• Since the Writing test is optional, you must register in advance in order to take it as part of the ACT.

• If you take it, you will do so after you complete the four multiple-choice subject tests.

The Format

The test consists of a single writing prompt that will define an issue and describe two points of view on that issue. You are asked to take a position on the issue, either by adopting one of the perspectives described or presenting a different point of view. State your position and support it with reasons and examples.

Read the directions now so that you do not need to take time to read them again during the test.

> Directions: *This is a test of your writing skills. You will have thirty (30) minutes to write an essay in English. Before you begin planning and writing your essay, read the writing prompt carefully to understand exactly what you are being asked to do. You essay will be evaluated on the evidence it provides of your ability to express judgments by taking a position on the issue in the writing prompt; to maintain a*

focus on the topic throughout the essay; to develop a position by using logical reasoning and by supporting your ideas; to organize ideas in a logical way; and to use language clearly and effectively according to the conventions of standard written English.

You may use the unlined pages in this test booklet to plan your essay. These pages will not be score. **You must write your essay in pencil on the lines pages in the answer folder.** *Your writings on those lined pages will be scored. You may not need all the lined pages, but to ensure you have enough room to finish, do NOT skip lines. You may write corrections or additions neatly between the lines of your essay, but do NOT write in the margins of the lined pages.* **Illegible essays cannot be scored, so you must write (or print) clearly.**

If you finish before time is called, you may review your work. Lay your pencil down immediately when time is called.

DO NOT OPEN THIS BOOKLET UNTIL TOLD TO DO SO.

Scoring

The writing test will not affect your scores on the multiple choice tests or your composite score. Rather, you will receive two additional scores: a combined English/Writing score on a scale of 1 through 36 and Writing subscore on a scale of 2 through 12.

Your essay will be judged on the following:

1. Clearly answering the question in the prompt;

2. Providing supporting evidence and reasoning;

3. Organization and no digressions;

4. Clear writing. Your essay should be simply stated and have no unnecessary words.

Tactic

Preparation

In the weeks before the test, refresh your memory about your favorite books, subjects, historical events, current events, and personal experiences.

Understand, Outline, and Organize

During the test, spend the first third of your time (about 10 minutes) understanding the prompt and deciding how you want to answer.

Know the questions that the prompt is asking. Take a position on the issue and state it clearly. Remember, there is no right or wrong position, you just need to be able to effectively support the position you do take.

As you jot down your ideas, include reasons and examples from literature, historical events, current events, and personal experience that support your point view. Also jot down what the

opposition might say and how you might rebut their argument. A bubble outline works well for this. Quickly organize your notes by numbering the order you want to express them.

Write

Spend about one-third of your time (about 10 minutes) writing your essay. Turn your notes into sentences and your sentences into paragraphs. Each paragraph should include the following:
1. Topic sentence
2. Support sentences
3. Transition sentence

The essay should be organized as follows:
1. Topic/thesis paragraph
2. Supporting paragraph
3. Supporting paragraph
4. Supporting paragraph
5. Concluding paragraph

Proofread

Spend the final third of your time proofreading your essay. Make corrections and revisions neatly and between the lines. Do not write in the margins. Correct your mistakes in the following areas:
1. Spelling
2. Grammar
3. Sentence structure

4. Punctuation

Practice

Practice writing different types of essays within 30 minutes. Practicing your essay writing will help you be better prepared for the Writing test.

The Week Before the Test

The week of the test, be sure to get plenty of rest, eat healthy, and stay hydrated. Consider the ACT test as the most important item on your schedule this week and decide how you will spend your time accordingly.

Wednesday/Thursday
1. Read General Tactics and the Tactics for each subject test.
2. Spend more time reviewing tactics for subjects and questions about which you feel less certain.
3. Identify the most difficult concepts for you in each subject. Spend more time reviewing these and working on several practice problems related to those concepts.
4. Review the types of questions that are most difficult for you and work on practice problems related to those types of questions.

Friday
1. DO NOT STUDY.
2. Do as little academics as possible.
3. Collect what you need to take to the test. Be sure to take the following items with you to the test center:
    - Watch or time piece
    - At least three sharpened No. 2 pencils
    - Pencil sharpener
    - Two erasers

- Photo ID card such as a Driver's License – make sure your ID is official
- Calculator
- Your admission ticket
- A high-protein snack – there is a break, and you might get hungry
- Directions to the testing site
4. Eat high protein meals.
5. Get a good night's sleep.

Saturday

1. Eat a high protein, but not heavy, breakfast.
2. Dress in layers.
3. Read something to wake up your brain.
4. Arrive early to the test.

Stop! Read on only if (a) you currently are a high school student or the parent of a high schooler; (b) your goal is to attend college; (c) contemplating the staggering cost of a four-year college induces within you strange physical symptoms such as loss of breath; or (d) any or all of the above.

If this describes you, take courage. Uncharted courses can appear daunting, but there is a roadway that will take you and your high schooler through choosing the best college, a marketable degree, and a fitting career path. So, put on your walking shoes and let's go!

Making Choices
The first step is actually to begin at the end and proceed backwards. It is easier to map a course when you know the destination. Choose a career or, if you are not yet ready to make that weighty decision, at least identify a life direction. God has a perfect plan for you, and that plan includes a life work. Parents, are the best person to guide your child in choosing a career or path. We have been students of our children since their births, observing their gifts, talents, and passions.

At age three, my son was intrigued with the drainage system in our neighborhood park. So I provided him with plenty of building toys and books about how things worked. It is no surprise he received a college degree in engineering. You can help your young adult discern his life's work by observing his talents, discussing his interests, and providing varied curricular and extracurricular activities.

A tangible step in choosing a career path is to take advantage of personality profile and career counseling resources. One such resource is www.collegeboard.myroad.com. It provides high schoolers with individualized personality profiles, career options,

and appropriate college majors. To confirm these results, look for opportunities to interview, shadow, or apprentice in your field of study.

What are the practice considerations of various career choices? How many hours are required to work each week? Would the salary support a family? How much travel would be involved? What about the job forecast? Are there any religious or moral issues to consider? An important step in choosing a career is to seek the counsel of others who know and love you. Most importantly, seek the Lord's direction through prayer. Once you have taken the first step of choosing a career or direction, you are ready to choose a college major.

What major area of study will best prepare you for your chosen field and make you marketable to future employees? My daughter enjoyed art and she chose a degree and career in graphic design as a marketable use of her skills.

Explore more about college majors through resources such as www.collgeboard.myroad.com, national magazines that evaluate colleges, such as *U.S. News and World Report* (www.usnews.com) and *The Princeton Review* (www.princetonreview.com), professional organizations, and college advisors. Once you have narrowed down the career choices and college studies, you are ready to select the college that will be the perfect fit.

Begin the process of choosing a university when you are is in your final two years of high school. Together, consider these important questions: Would I best thrive in a public or private college? Is a private school important to us? Would I flourish at a larger university with many diverse opportunities, or would a small, personal college be the place where I would best grow? Would I be more comfortable in a metropolis, suburban, or rural setting?

What about the distance from home?

Explore the admission requirements, and don't forget the cost and available financial aid. After you have determined your parameters, select six to eight schools that fit within those guidelines and request general college information and specific departmental information from them. Spend time browsing through materials with the goal of limiting your selection to the top three or four schools.

Colleges are academically ranked in three tiers. Unless you rest soundly on one extreme of the academic continuum, you should consider selecting a tier I university, one to three tier II schools, and one tier III college. Next, visit as many of these universities as possible. Take a list of questions, be sure to visit the admissions and financial aid offices, take a campus tour, check out the housing options, and make an appointment with a faculty member. Alternatively, attend college fairs in your area where you can speak with a representative from the university.

Once you have completed the steps of choosing a career, deciding upon a major, and selecting a college, you will have completed the first leg of your path from high school to college. You can now confidently select the best high school course of study.

Planning High School
Now that you know where you are headed, the next stretch of the course is to map out a high school plan. High school transcripts must not only meet the mandates of your state's high school graduation requirements, but also the admission requisites of prospective universities, the recommendations of the college or department major within the university, and your desires.

The demands of these four entities often differ. Our state does not

mandate foreign language for high school graduation. However, all of the universities to which my children applied required two years of foreign language in high school. Similarly our state required only three years of math and science and several universities had the same regulations, but the colleges of engineering wanted four years of both high school math and science, while my daughter's college of graphic design required only two. The assorted requirements may be obtained through your school's guidance counselor, the state educational organization, the admissions department of your prospective university, and the department or "college" of your prospective major.

College admissions applications will require high school transcripts, scores from college entrance exams, academic honors, community involvement, leadership experience, letters of recommendations, work, and extracurricular experiences.

Paying for College
Financing higher education is the home stretch of your journey from high school to college. Knowing the course in this area can help you finish strong and save dollars. One of the most common ways to cut costs is to attend a local community college. Some community colleges offer concurrent enrollment programs whereby students can receive both high school and college credit for the same course. As much as two years of undergraduate work can be completed at a community college, saving money on tuition, room, and board.

If you choose this route, beware of a few potential pitfalls. First, not all credits earned through a community college will transfer to your chosen four-year university. Second, too many credit hours earned through a community college may disqualify your student from scholarships, grants, and other money offered to only to

incoming freshmen. Ignorance of these potential snares may ultimately cost you more than you save.

You can bypass thousands of college dollars by taking the right tests in high school. The PSAT (Preliminary Scholastic Aptitude Test) is used as a college scholarship indicator as well as a qualifier for the National Merit Scholarship Program. The PSAT is taken in the fall of the student's junior year. A National Merit Scholar may receive a tuition waiver from a prospective college. Many universities offer handsome scholarships to those who score high enough to be named a commendable scholar, semi-finalist, or finalist.

Even if your high schooler's score does not qualify him for these rewards, it can be used to identify weak areas before taking the SAT. Most colleges require scores from the ACT or SAT as part of the admission process. However, sufficiently high scores on these tests can also qualify your student for merit-based scholarships. The best time to take the ACT or SAT is the end of the high school junior year. Scores from tests taken in the fall of the senior year will still be received in time for college admission applications. Consider our ACT Prep Guide and online tutoring. Visit www.purplechalkboard.com for more information.

Two other tests can help you save money by testing out of college classes while still in high school. If you take the Advanced Placement (AP) exams and score high enough, you can apply these course credits toward freshman year at college. Approximately 23 subject exams are offered, costing $70 to $80 each and scored on a 1-5 scale. The CLEP (College Level Examination Program) may also give advanced standing. These exams cost $50 each and cover various subjects. Scores range from 20 to 80, and many colleges require students to score a 50 to 60 for advanced standing.

You can save time and money by understanding how the AP and CLEP exams differ. The greatest variance is in content. The CLEP is designed for any student with a proper understanding of the subject. AP exams are fashioned from the AP course outline, and achieving the desired score may be challenging without first taking an AP course. This can be overcome by using the AP outline along with your high school course or by obtaining an AP subject prep book from your local book-store. A second difference is that while both tests have multiple-choice questions, most AP exams also include essay questions. Many colleges will award advanced standing through AP, but fewer will do so through CLEP. Finally, AP exams are offered only in May and only through local high schools. CLEP exams are offered on more than 2,900 college campuses and can be taken at any time. My son took three AP exams his senior year and achieved the desired score on only one. Although we spent $240 on three AP tests, by passing one test, he saved $5,000 in college tuition. My daughter tested out of an entire year of courses through AP and CLEP tests, saving us over $10,000.

Financial assistance in the form of merit scholarships, need-based scholarships, grants, work-study, and loans can be obtained through federal, state, and local programs, as well as from your prospective college. The U.S. Department of Education will award approximately 70 billion dollars in federal aid this year to help families afford the towering cost of higher education. Completing the Free Application for Federal Student Aid (FAFSA) is the first step in receiving federal financial aid. The initial FAFSA is submitted after January 1 and before June 30 during your student's high school senior year. Federal Pell Grants and Federal Supplemental Educational opportunity Grants (FSEOG) are both calculated from the information provided on the FAFSA.

Pell Grants are designed for undergraduate students who have

not yet received a college degree. If you have an extreme need, you may also be eligible for a FSEOG. Neither grant needs to be repaid. The FAFSA determines your eligibility for other needs-based financial aid programs.

Federal work-study is a campus-based program that provides on-campus jobs for students with demonstrated financial need. Typically the wage is minimum. A Stafford Loan is a loan to the student, while PLUS Loans are loans to the parents of dependent college children. Federal Perkins Loans are campus-based, low-interest loans available to undergraduate and graduate students. Not only is the FAFSA a requirement for all federal aid, but it is also mandatory for most state and college aid, and state deadlines for submitting FAFSA may be earlier than the federal deadline.

Individual states can provide great benefits. Every state offers money for college through various state-sponsored scholarship programs, grants, and prepaid tuition plans. In our home state of Oklahoma, for instance, the State Regents for Higher Education offers merit scholarships from $1000 per year up to a full, four-year college ride. Find the information relevant to your state by contacting the state higher education office.

Nearly every college has its own scholarship and grant programs. Some awards are determined by FAFSA; others require separate application. Ask your prospective college for a financial aid brochure. After the freshman year, numerous departmental scholarships are also available for the asking.

Don't ignore smaller awards offered locally. "Smaller" can mean any amount between $100 and $10,000. To locate these scholarships, contact your local government representative, your public library, or search the Internet. You may not think to turn to organizations for help with college costs, even though they are

some of the best sources. These magnanimous organizations include service groups such as the Elks Club and Boy Scouts of America. They also include foundations formed by corporations or individuals that give away roughly 7,000 scholarships annually worth $45 million. Professional organizations, trade unions, and military service organizations also fall under this category. Don't forget to inquire about scholarships offered by your church, employer, or trade organization.

Other places you may not think to look are military colleges and ROTC. All three branches of the Armed Services operate their own degree-granting academies where a student can receive a "free" academically superior college education in exchange for the opportunity to serve his country after graduation. One of my children choose this path; his college was fully paid for and he received a stipend each month.

Athletic scholarships are currently a popular possibility, and work well for some. Consider the costs of this avenue before investing the colossal amount of time required to win an athletic scholarship. First, consider the possibility of physical injury that can take you out of the running for an athletic scholarship. Second, assuming you land that full scholarship, consider the time commitment required for playing college sports while attending college.

Ladies and gentlemen, we've now come to the end of our guided tour from career choice to major to college, from application to activities to aid. I hope you've enjoyed your stroll and that it has helped to prepare you for the real promenade. Have a pleasant journey!

www.ingramcontent.com/pod-product-compliance
Lightning Source LLC
Chambersburg PA
CBHW080738300426
44114CB00019B/2625